Biblical Faith and the Black American

Latta R. Thomas

Judson Press • Valley Forge

BIBLICAL FAITH AND THE BLACK AMERICAN

Copyright © 1976
Judson Press, Valley Forge, PA 19481

Unless otherwise indicated, Bible quotations in this volume are in accordance with the Revised Standard Version of the Bible, copyrighted 1952 and 1971 by the Division of Christian Education of the National Council of the Churches of Christ in the United States of America, and are used by permission.

Other versions of the Bible quoted in this book are:

The Holy Bible, King James Version (KJV).

Good News for Modern Man (TEV), The New Testament and Psalms in Today's English Version. Copyright © American Bible Society, 1966, 1970, 1971.

Library of Congress Cataloging in Publication Data

Thomas, Latta R.
  Biblical faith and the Black American.
  Bibliography: p. 153.
  Includes index.
  1. Bible—Criticism, interpretation, etc.
2. Afro-Americans—Religion. 3. Freedom
(Theology)—Biblical teaching. I. Title.
BS511.2.T48   220.6   76-13640
ISBN 0-8170-0718-0

Printed in the U.S.A. ⊕

God in his Providence has mitigated the hard roads in my life by the quality of traveling companions he has allowed me. Some of these I met but briefly yet meaningfully, while with others I have spent many fruitful years. Some have passed on; a few are still sharing with me their wisdom and encouragement.

Therefore I dedicate this work not to one but to several who were and are my teachers, mentors, and inspirers even when they do not or did not know it. The list of those who steadied me consists of:

Rev. A. A. Sims
Mrs. Ethel G. Sims
Mrs. Grace Holt
Rev. H. H. Battle
Rev. William P. Diggs, Sr.
Dr. Maxie S. Gordon, Sr.
Dr. Lincoln C. Jenkins, Sr.
Dr. Charles H. Brown
Dr. E. S. Rutherford
Dr. James R. Branton
Dr. Oren H. Baker
Dr. W. E. Saunders

Dr. Winthrop S. Hudson
Dr. Nels F. S. Ferré
Dr. J. Earl Thompson, Jr.
Dr. Harvey Cox
Prof. Gayraud Wilmore
Dr. Lucius M. Tobin
Dr. Gardner C. Taylor
Dr. Eddie O'Neal
Dr. Edmund Holt Linn
Dr. Meredith Handspicker
Dr. Joseph E. O'Donnell

Foreword

While there may be a number of well-qualified persons to write on religion and the Black American, no one is more qualified than Latta Thomas. And no one could be more honored than I to have been asked to write this Foreword. For the past two decades, I have known Latta as a friend, as a fellow seminarian at the Colgate-Rochester Divinity School, and, more recently, as a faculty colleague at Benedict College in Columbia, South Carolina. Still more recently, I have been privileged to watch this book grow as an extension of the personality of a man whose persistent and incisive biblical scholarship combine with a liberating faith and a firsthand knowledge of the Black experience in America.

The voice that speaks in these pages is the voice of a respected scholar and honored teacher of philosophy and religion whose ability to reach the minds of students is obvious on the college campus where Professor Thomas has served for many years. It is also the voice of Pastor Thomas whose love for the church is confirmed by a lifetime of faithful service. It is also the voice of Chaplain Thomas whose message of God's declaration of war on human oppression and exploitation has sounded with courageous regularity in college chapel and parish congregation. It is finally, and perhaps most importantly, the voice of the *man,* Latta Thomas, whose passionate commitment to a liberating God burns through the "color-line" to rend the veil of racism that W. E. B. DuBois prophetically declared "the problem of the Twentieth Century."

The real power of *Biblical Faith and the Black American* lies deeper than its clear articulation of a sound biblical theology for Black liberation. While the author rightly addresses his Black brothers and sisters to rediscover the Bible in a "liberation time," the author himself has been *addressed by* a Word that speaks through the suffering and enslaved to call *all* Americans to a new freedom-in-obedience. I, as a White American, hear that Word in this book, and I have heard it repeatedly in the life of Latta Thomas. Therefore, while I share the author's hope that his words will reach the souls of Black folk, I must add my own hope that they will reach beyond as well.

The distinguished Black American writer, Ralph Ellison, concludes his novel, *Invisible Man,* with a penetrating question. He creates a modern epic of a young Black man's search for his own freedom and identity, and he concludes by having his protagonist ask: "Who knows but that, on the lower frequencies, I speak for you?"[1] Such a question might appropriately be added to Latta Thomas's *Biblical Faith and the Black American.* If it were, my own answer would be: "He *does!*"

Jerold J. Savory
Chairman, English Department
Columbia College
Columbia, South Carolina

[1] Ralph Ellison, *Invisible Man* (New York: Random House, Inc., 1952), p. 439.

Acknowledgments

The thoughts on these pages have been mine in less organized form since my teen years. I gratefully acknowledge, however, that the opportunity to give order to my thinking came from the combined generosity of the American Baptist Student Aid Fund, Andover Newton Theological Seminary, and Benedict College whose financial help and encouragement enabled me to return to school in 1973.

I owe a debt of gratitude also to persons who dedicated themselves to the tedious clerical tasks, among whom were: Mrs. Manatha Young, of the Benedict College faculty; her student assistant, Miss Jacqueline Williams; Miss Geraldine Snipes, secretary to the Deputy Director of the South Carolina Department of Youth Services; Miss Charlotte Grooms and Mrs. Joyce Seabrook, from the clerical staff of Student Affairs at Benedict College.

In addition, my thanks goes to Dr. Jerold Savory, Chairman, Department of English, Columbia College, Columbia, South Carolina, who has aided me not only through his literary expertise but also by his years of close friendship. His direction with reference to the manuscript and publication procedure has been very valuable.

Of course, the appreciation I feel for the members of my family, my wife and two sons, is hardly expressible. Their faith and anticipation kept me diligent.

Latta R. Thomas
Department of Religion and Philosophy
Benedict College

Contents

Introduction

In most Black American communities today, liberation, self-determination, healthy identity, and justice for Black people are the main items on the agenda. Concern for the well-being of Black people does not automatically rule out concern for the well-being of all people, for, as well-informed Black leaders point out, as the lot of people farthest down is improved, all people benefit. But with the present situation of Blacks being on the bottom rung of the social, economic, political, and educational ladder, the primary effort must be directed toward them. In any case, this is the thinking in most Black communities.

The people in these communities are saying that all other efforts and concerns must be suspended until Black people are totally liberated. Whatever contributes to that liberation is good; whatever either obstructs this effort or is irrelevant to it is evil. Everything the Black person embraces or deals with, they say, must be questioned, tested, and rated in the light of whether it helps or hinders Black liberation, no matter whether these be political theory, economic systems, philosophies, or religions.

In this same sense, many Black people are raising very searching questions about the Bible. They want to know if it affirms and supports Black liberation. Many of them wonder if the Bible is not just another tool in the hands of Whites, used to keep Black people blind, quiet, and dependent in a society which is against them. People who are expressing these suspicions and hostilities are not limited to the ranks of the poor and uneducated Blacks. Some who are highly trained and economically well-off are just as loud and passionate in expressing their feeling that the Bible works against Black liberation. The attitudes of Muslim converts, many Black college intellectuals and students, and Black professionals attest to this eroding suspicion and hostility.

To understand this wave of Black hostility toward the Bible, one needs to give deep thought to the fact that for several centuries in Western countries the Bible has been *used*—and to a degree still is— as an instrument for supporting Black oppression and exploitation as will later be shown. But the devilish irony of the matter is that a collection of writings whose general content condemns war and human enslavement, oppression, and exploitation was twisted and distorted through faulty interpretation and made to support and justify human oppression.

In reality the Bible, when allowed to come through without human tampering by people with shallow minds and evil motives, not only *does not* support human oppression, but also *urges human rebellion* against mistreatment of human beings as a matter of commitment to the God of heaven, earth, and history. But the biblical message does not remain satisfied with that. It further affirms that top priority must be given to securing the well-being of the weak, helpless, oppressed, and enslaved. The author of the book of Exodus asserted that God commissioned Moses to lead Israel, a slave-labor colony, to freedom from Egyptian bondage. The Gospel writer, Luke, represented Jesus as saying in the parable of the lost sheep that the shepherd left the ninety-nine sheep in the pen and searched untiringly for one sheep which was lost. And the central theme of the New Testament is that God himself came to man's hopeless and helpless situation (incarnation) to lift human beings from the condition characterized by human sin and misery, and through Jesus the Christ began his work with those farthest down—the have-nots, the enslaved, the outcasts, the wounded, and the "nobodies" of this world.

The purpose of these pages, therefore, is to reach the minds and hearts of Black people in America inside and outside of the Black church who would like to see in the biblical tradition at least a measure of what many of their foreparents discerned in it but who have some honest doubts and suspicions due to the ways the Bible has been misinterpreted and manipulated to support Black oppression. The greatest tragedy that could happen to Black people in a day when full liberation is the password is to have them pass up the greatest collective document of human liberation that has ever come out of human experience and the effort of God. Black people must find out for themselves, especially in these days, what the Bible is really about. For it is a book in which it is recorded that *the* God and Sovereign of all history is always in the business of creating and freeing a people to clear the earth of injustice, bigotry, hatred, human slavery, political corruption, tyranny, sin, illness, and poverty. It is a book in which there is an invitation to all people who will hear and respond to put all else aside and join God in the job of renewing the earth, believing that it *must* and *can* be done.

Everything that follows in this book is founded on these basic beliefs or convictions.

1. The Bible is through and through a collective document which grew out of and is about God's liberation of people from human sin and human oppression, and true liberation is made real on earth when oppressed people and those who throw in their lot with them *hear* and *act* on the call of God to rebel against the evil in the world, accepting God's direction and power.

2. The Bible pictures the real God of heaven and earth and of Jesus Christ as *always* concentrating his liberating efforts and concerns where human beings are in need, being mistreated, and held down;[1] that God is doing the same thing here and now where Black people are being held under by racism,* brutality, poverty, and inadequate schools.

3. Before the Bible can be seen in all its liberating purity and power, the effort must be made to identify and cut through those motives, myths,* and interpretations, whether deliberate or accidental, which resulted in the attempts to twist the Bible in support of Black enslavement and white racism.

4. Black people, particularly in America but actually everywhere,

---

[1] Cf. Walter Rauschenbusch, *The Social Principles of Jesus* (Philadelphia: American Baptist Publication Society, 1916).

*Terms followed by an asterisk are defined in the Glossary at the back of the book.

need the liberating power and direction available in the biblical faith as never before, and should fully embrace them; therefore the Black pastor, the Black church, the Black youth, and even the Black intellectual need not stand in paralyzing shame or frustrating hatred before the document in which their foreparents discerned so much strength and hope, but rather should embrace it as the foundation of today's Black church in America

The hope is that Black persons who are earnestly concerned about Black liberation may find in these pages some encouragement to examine the Bible for themselves, this time without the distortions and misinterpretations of racists, and thus rediscover its relevance and power for Black liberation. But keep in mind always that mind as well as devotion and hard effort as well as fervent prayer must be applied to dig out the gold of the Bible's liberating message. When one sets out to learn anything that is or may be important, one must, to some good degree, consult the works and judgments of people who have spent a lot of time and effort learning facts about the matter. This is called study or research. Every important matter deserves study if the truth about it is to be passed on to someone else.

In the same way, the Bible, if Black people feel that it is or may be important, needs to be studied or researched. This does not mean that a person who studies or researches the Bible is an atheist or an infidel. On the contrary, such a person usually feels that the Bible is so important that special effort ought to be made to find out as much as possible about it so that no mistakes will be visited upon it.

Again study and research are necessary for knowing the Bible for another reason. The various documents or books or letters which make up the Bible are all several centuries old. They deal with and interpret people and events of the times in which they were written. Therefore, a standing rule in understanding and interpreting the Bible is to find out by research what a book or passage in the Bible "meant" when it was first written, before one goes on to tell people today what it "means" now. Much of the trouble in biblical interpretation has resulted from bypassing this rule either out of ignorance or bias. There were some people who just did not know any better; there were others who wanted to twist the Bible into saying what they already wanted it to say. In both cases the all-important rule was ignored.

In an effort to offer some modest degree of help to Black people who wish to see the Bible as it is in all its liberating power, the following path will be taken. The first look will be at some of the ways racists attempted to twist and use the Bible and why they did it. Emphasis will then shift to the correct method of understanding and treating biblical literature so that the biblical faith is allowed to greet, challenge, liberate, and empower those who commit themselves to it. Next, the Old Testament will be examined for some selected liberation relevance points, such as the sacred legend* of Cain and Abel, the books of Ruth, Daniel, Jonah, Job, Exodus, and some of the Hebrew Prophets.

Then the New Testament will be surveyed with emphasis on Jesus and Paul, though not exclusively, to show how the thrust of their concerns identifies with today's struggle for Black liberation and wholeness. Attention will then move to a task which the author has long felt needs to be taken up, that of recasting or reinterpreting where necessary, and eliminating where needed, several concepts which have become closely associated with the biblical faith. The measuring rod for doing this is today's burning agenda of Black liberation. There will be examined the concepts of sin, personal piety, otherworldliness,* the doctrine of world abandonment,* and the kingdom of God. * The question will be raised as to what do or should these concepts mean to Black people today in view of the real biblical message.

The concluding chapter will be a word of encouragement and caution to the Black church which in its agony, labor, and service has had to endure barbs and negative criticisms from both Whites and Blacks and often undeservedly. Many of those criticisms came from those who had neither the moral and ethical credentials nor a firsthand knowledge as a basis for judgment.

At the end of the book will be a short glossary of some terms which may not be too familiar to the nontechnical reader. Asterisks (*) mark those words and terms which will be listed in alphabetical order and explained at the end of the book.

Also at the end of each chapter will be some questions growing out of that chapter. It is hoped that these will encourage and stimulate the reader toward further thought and study.

The Bible and Black Experience

When Black folk were first brought against their will to the shores of what later was called the United States of America, they were introduced to drudgery, brutality, and distorted driblets of biblical interpretation. More often than not these bits of interpretation were shaped to make sure that the Blacks who absorbed them would become and remain the mental, emotional, and physical slaves of the owners of the plantations on which they resided.

But Divine Providence is always steps ahead of human stratagems. Joseph's brothers may sell their kin; yet they can never control or determine the consequences and circumstances which flow from or in spite of their actions. Yes, as the will of the God of history, of Abraham, Isaac, and Jacob, of Moses, Elijah, Isaiah, and Amos, of John and Jesus brought it to pass, Black people were able to penetrate the biblical distortions and misinterpretations and discern the real biblical message of human liberation and wholeness.

The Miracle of It All

This is the amazing thing—that Blacks were able to see themselves and the power of a liberating God in the stories and models of Moses, Daniel, Joshua, the three Hebrew boys in the fiery furnace, John, and

Jesus. They identified with those heroes of faith and daring and perceived that the same God who empowered them was available and active in their midst as well. They created songs to celebrate these convictions. We now call them spirituals and congregational songs. Not only that, those Black toilers in the heat of the day created a biblical theology, long before Bultmann, with "Sweet Jesus" as the center. Jesus, the Redeemer and Liberator, was the Lily of the Valley, the Rose of Sharon, the Bright and Morning Star. He was a Bridge over deep waters, a Ladder over high mountains, Water in dry places, and Bread in a starving land.

It is no accident, therefore, that the early American Black church in bullrush exile produced a Nat Turner, a Gabriel Prosser, a Denmark Vessey, a David Walker, a Sojourner Truth, a Harriet Tubman, to say nothing of such persons as Richard Allen, Absalom Jones, Alexander Crummell, Henry Highland Garnet, Martin R. Delany, and Frederick Douglass.

All of these saw the real biblical message and the redemptive and liberating God shining through it. They, in spite of the demonic efforts to prevent it, discerned that the Bible was the document proclaiming the sovereign God of all history whose whole thrust is against human oppression and misery. Yet the sad and pitiful irony of it all is that many of their children today do not see what they saw and, therefore, have not the power, guidance, hope, and sustenance which they had.

Black people, for whatever reasons, today could very well bypass the one source of motivation, inspiration, power, and guidance which not even systemic and systematic racism can take away from them, the Bible. The reasons for present Black suspicion of the biblical faith are complex, many, and varied. Yet, the main reason seems to be that too many Blacks today have believed too much and too little about the Bible at the same time. That is, many have been gullible to faulty beliefs and statements on the one hand and have rejected worthwhile convictions on the other.

For instance, some Black people have swallowed, cat-fish style, so to speak, the faulty assumptions of many uninformed opponents of the Bible. One often hears that the Bible is the White European's book; that the Judeo-Christian faith based on the Bible is of necessity pro-White and anti-Black; and that being for the Bible means that you must be for the D.A.R., the John Birch Society, the Ku Klux Klan, and the elimination of welfare. The above assertions are simply not true. It is a fact that often the Bible has been and is misinterpreted, misused, and distorted; yet suppose we eliminate every potentially good thing in this world which has been similarly abused. We would soon see the folly of such a course of action.

In addition, the gullibility just mentioned has been compounded by the easy acceptance in another direction. Too many contemporary Blacks have adopted with little question the assertions of the misinformed and bigoted "friends" of the Bible who teach that the Bible advocated Black slavery and racial segregation; advocated that religious piety consists of personal, private, and other worldly aspects only; and teach that the "big" sins are the consumption of alcohol and cigarettes, sexual expressions, dancing, and frolicking. This set of faulty assumptions about what the Bible says misses the mark as much as did the first.

For the biblical faith declares war on human oppression, self-centeredness, escapism, and greed. It declares from Genesis to Revelation that the chief human sin is attempting to take God's seat, like Lucifer, and to play the role of God over one's neighbor.

But at the same time some Black sons and daughters reject and still push aside their foreparents' experience of the biblical God. In the book of divine-human encounter, Blacks of yesteryears experienced God as the *Mysterium Tremendum**whose awe-inspiring presence gave strength for another week; who acted in liberation evoking the poetic expressions that he "moves in mysterious ways, his wonders to perform," that he would "make a way out of no way." He was a God who admonished his followers to be alert in their allegiance to his work on earth as they sang to the model of the wise virgins, "Have oil in your vessels, your lamps trimmed and burning; Be ready when the Bridegroom comes!" or "I want to be ready to walk into Jerusalem just like John." This faith Blacks rejected but should have embraced for themselves.

The point now is that just as our Black foreparents encountered the biblical God and received strength for survival and liberation in their time, we, their children, must rediscover that same resource for Black liberation in the measure demanded today.

To bring about this rediscovery requires some knowledge of how the Bible has been misused, how to rectify that misuse and release the real liberating biblical message, and how to understand biblical revelation. The rest of this chapter is given to the task of contribution in some measure to that knowledge.

Freedom of Speech Denied to God in America—Eisegesis

Minorities and poor folks have not been the only ones denied freedom of speech in America over the decades. God himself has been and is being denied freedom of speech at various points and by various groups and persons in this country. In Christian circles the Bible is (or contains or mediates) the "Word" or the communication of God to human beings; yet this form of communication from the Divine has been and still is being diluted, distorted, and misinterpreted at many points in the country. In that sense God himself has been and is being denied freedom of speech by those who prevent the real biblical message from coming through.

But unlike the method of forcing silence upon disinherited humans, the tactic used to abridge God's freedom of speech has been and is to put words into God's mouth, so to speak. Human beings have tried to do this for a long time, for several reasons. One reason is that many human creatures like to appear to be able to guess or predict the actions of God. Still another reason people put words into God's mouth is that they fear that what God is really saying just may be contrary to what they wish him to say. The late, venerable American preacher, Harry Emerson Fosdick, clearly pointed out the dangers which are possible from this ego trip of human beings who try to read their ideas "into" the Bible.[1]

The danger resulting from reading one's own notions, ideas, and preferences into the Bible is so demonic and harmful that one cannot warn people about it too much. For when a human being, imperfect and inclined to sin, reads his or her notions, ideas, and preferences into the biblical message, he or she is very likely to read into it his or her prejudices, biases, and animosities. The sons and daughters of Adam often attempt to hide from the real voice of God.

Eisegesis and How It Works

This reading "into" God's Word has caused biblical scholars to coin the word "eisegesis" from the Greek word *eis,* which means "into" and *hegesthai* which means "lead." Under no circumstances should one eisegete, regardless of the temporary advantage or expediency which such may satisfy. Do not eisegete to win an argument over biblical interpretation. Do not eisegete even to preach

---

[1] Harry Emerson Fosdick, *The Modern Use of the Bible* (New York: The Macmillan Company, 1958), pp. 36-37; 87-90.

rousing sermons, as valuable and needed as a good, lively sermon is. The use of the correct setting of the biblical passage is just as powerful, and it does not make God seem to lie.

What are some of the practices which open the door to eisegesis and create loopholes through which people attempt to put words into God's mouth? The four most notable eisegeting practices are as follows. One is that of proof-texting. This practice follows the procedure of plucking various verses or statements in the Bible out of context and placing them together arbitrarily to "prove" some (usually preconceived) point. An example is the atheist* who declared that he could prove that the Bible condoned suicide. He took the passage from Matthew 27:5, "And throwing down the pieces of silver in the temple, he departed; and he went and hanged himself," and placed beside it the one from Luke 10:37, "And Jesus said to him, 'Go and do likewise.'"

It is obvious to the most casual Bible reader that the two contexts are different. The first passage related Judas's remorse. The second has reference to Jesus' admonition at the end of the parable of the good Samaritan. Yet this usage is indicative of much of the naiveté which is brought to the Bible often to "prove" some previously held belief. Also this kind of thinking has behind it, in most cases, a semi-magical concept of the Bible—that words, sentences, and verses are sacred in and of themselves "because" they are found between the biblical covers.

A second eisegetical practice is overspiritualizing, perhaps the sneakiest of them all. It employs the method of taking passages and references in the Bible which have to do with objects, events, places, and persons of this world and declaring that these passages and references do not deal with this world but with some otherworldly, spiritual, and unseen realm. To the overspiritualizer this concrete world lies beyond the concern of the God of the Bible. Such a one feels that God's creation is somehow a necessary evil at best, and that human involvement in the attempt to eliminate social injustice, poverty, oppression, ignorance, war, and disease is questionable and useless. In other words the overspiritualizer, notwithstanding his or her lip service, does not take seriously either the incarnation or the Hebraic-Christian concept of creation which declares God's handiwork to be "very good" (Genesis 1:31). To the overspiritualizer, God's redemption is reduced from covering the whole person to soul saving only.

Yet, the pain of it all is that sometimes even reputable biblical scholars overspiritualize. Following is an example. It is or should be generally known that people in the Black church committed to the task of Black liberation have found a tremendous amount of theological meaning and support in Luke 4:16-21 which reports that Jesus in a synagogue service read Isaiah 61:1-2*a* and applied the passage to his redemptive and liberating mission under God. James H. Cone, the brilliant, Black theologian, has declared this passage to be of central revelatory value; so have many other noted Black church people. It reads: "Then Jesus went to Nazareth, where he had been brought up, and on the Sabbath day he went as usual to the synagogue. He stood up to read the Scriptures, and was handed the book of the prophet Isaiah. He unrolled the scroll and found the place where it is written:

'The Spirit of the Lord is upon me,
because he has chosen me to preach the
Good News to the poor.
He has sent me to *proclaim liberty to the captives,*
    and *recovery of sight to the blind;*
To set free the oppressed,
and announce *the year* when the Lord
will *save his people!'*

"Jesus rolled up the scroll, gave it back to the attendant, and sat down. All the people in the synagogue had their eyes fixed on him. He began speaking to them: 'This passage of scripture has come true today, as you heard it being read!'" (TEV, italics added.)

Now to continue the example of how even reputable biblical scholars overspiritualize, let us compare the scholarly treatment of Isaiah 61:1-2 done by one writer and that of Luke 4:16-21 done by another scholar—both treatments appearing in the reputable work *The Interpreter's One-Volume Commentary on the Bible.* The interesting result of the comparison was that it turned out to be a contrast. Peter R. Ackroyd of England, the Old Testament scholar treating Isaiah, drew one conclusion while William Baird of the U.S.A., the New Testament expert dealing with Luke 4, expressed a different opinion.

A closer glance indicated which scholar overspiritualized. Ackroyd said of Isaiah 61:1-2*a:*

Liberty to the captives suggests the law governing the release of slaves at the end of a 6-year period (Exod. 21:1-6) rather than the more elaborate jubilee (Lev. 25); **proclaim the year of . . . favor** perhaps suggests a proclamation made at the beginning of such a year of release. But the terminology may well be metaphorical, and shows a particular type of *interpretation of the Exile,** not altogether unlike that in Lev. 26:34; II Chr. 36:21. *It is a period of slavery from which release is offered;* now the day of hope dawns, the **day** of divine "rescue" or "requital," rather than **vengeance** (vs. 2*b*).[2]

William Baird's commentary on part of the Lukan passage says this:

> The surprising thing is Jesus' interpretation. **Today this scripture has been fulfilled in your hearing** means that Jesus understands his own mission as fulfilling the ancient prophecy. He is the one **anointed . . . to preach good news to the poor;** his baptism was the event of his anointing with the Spirit. *Jesus is the one who will proclaim release to the captives and recovering of sight to the blind. The latter anticipates Jesus' ministry of physical healing, whereas the former, along with the declaration* that he will *set at liberty those who are oppressed, refers to Jesus' ability to cast out the demons who hold men in bondage.*[3]

The italics are to aid the contrast.

The reader will note closely that Ackroyd, the Old Testament scholar, is clear in his insistence that the writer of Isaiah 61 had human slaves in mind, flesh-and-blood human beings who were held in physical bondage by other human beings. He indicates that there may be some debate as to whether the prophet was referring to the six-year Hebrew slave period or to the Exile. But regardless of the reference, here is meant concrete instances of human bondage sustained by humans.

In spite of the above commentary and New Testament Greek, Baird writes that Jesus meant by "setting at liberty those who are oppressed" or enslaved that he was freeing people from "demons." * New Testament Greek terminology in that passage does not indicate "demons." The Greek term for demon is *daimonion* and does not appear in the passage. The Greek term which does appear is *aichmalotos* which means a human being held against his will by another human being, not by a demon.

Baird here has overspiritualized, and seemingly several assumptions drove him to do so. He assumed, in spite of the weight of Old Testament scholarship, that the writer of Second Isaiah* was

---

[2] Charles M. Laymon, ed., *The Interpreter's One-Volume Commentary on the Bible* (Nashville: Abingdon Press, 1971), p. 368 (italics mine).

[3] *Ibid.,* p. 680, italics added.

referring to some highly spiritualized or nonworldly order. Or he assumed that while the prophet was speaking about concrete conditions of slavery, Jesus radically changed the interpretation of the passage. And this writer highly suspects that Baird assumed that Jesus was rather insensitive to the social injustices of his day.

A third error which admits eisegesis is arbitrary allegorizing. This fault is embodied in the practice of saying without a scholarly basis that a difficult passage has a secret or mysterious meaning hidden in an allegory* and then giving one's personal interpretation of the assumed allegory. To be sure, there are some allegories in the Bible. But it is to do grave injury to biblical interpretation to declare allegories where there are none. Such a practice is a clear road to wild and irresponsible personal commentaries and thus invites eisegesis. Quite often millenarian*, sectarian, and modern apocalyptic* groups thrive on this practice, using such biblical books as Genesis, Daniel, Ezekiel, and Revelation.

Still a fourth blunder, very widespread in its contamination, which leads to the eisegetical traps is literalizing. This error rides piggyback on the belief that everything written in the Bible must be regarded as referring to literal, historical events and descriptions of concrete or "five-sense" objects. It is amazing how some people will agree in a Bible study class that the Bible contains poetry and parable as well as history and in the next half hour insist that the serpent in Eden talked, that Jonah lived undigested in the belly of a whale for three days, and that three men literally walked in an overheated furnace.

At first glance, literalizing may not appear to leave the door open to eisegesis. But further thought on the matter will soon reveal that such a practice makes it easy for one to do two things, both of which will lead to eisegesis. First, it leads to a compartmentalization of life into a religious fantasy on one side and reality on the other. A person will then use eisegetical myths in an attempt to glue the two worlds together. The other result of literalism leading to eisegetical whim is the tendency to insist that religiously and spiritually "the good old days" are gone and the likes will never be experienced again. There will never be any more Daniels who will be God-filled enough to walk into a den of lions, they insist. Now this is eisegesis on the grandest scale. The God who reveals himself in the biblical record, in Jesus Christ, and in the Holy Spirit is the living God, who is not only Alpha but also Omega, who is the Eternal, and who is not the God of the dead past but of the living and liberating present and future.

Therefore any tendency or claim which relegates God's power solely to the past walks hand-in-hand with eisegesis.

Therefore let the reader beware of the muses of eisegesis—proof-texting, overspiritualizing, arbitrary allegorizing, and literalizing. Their victims are many and their influence deadly. This brings us to the central purpose of this chapter: namely, to show how many White racists in America eisegeted the liberating biblical message in order to support Black slavery and racial segregation and discrimination; and to show what counter measure must be taken and what facts must be learned to tap the liberating power of the genuine biblical message.

Some Examples of How Racists in America Eisegete

As contradictory and schizoid as it may sound, there were and are in America White churchmen and churchwomen, emotionally adamant in their claim to be Christian and loyal to the Bible, who believed that God not only permitted human slavery, racial discrimination, and segregation to be directed against Blacks but also that he actually willed and planned such structures. No doubt, there were some Whites in this country who sought religious and philosophical justifications for Black slavery and racial discrimination and segregation out of greed and vested interest, but there were many more who out of their biblical teachings and theological indoctrinations earnestly believed that the Bible taught that Blacks should be the slaves of White people by divine decree. The background of that decree, as the argument went, was that God, at one point in human history, had laid a curse upon the progenitor or forefather of all Black people in the world, and from that day forward all Blacks were to be "hewers of wood and drawers of water."

This argument was and is known as the Ham Doctrine. The set of beliefs involved grew out of a rather shrewd eisegesis of Genesis 9:20-27. Built on the assumptions (1) that the story of Noah and his sons was historical; (2) that Ham was Black; and (3) that God agreed with Noah in his bestowal of the curse; this conviction was preached and taught in White churches. It wielded perennial influence, and its devotees are not all dead today.

It ought to be further pointed out that such a doctrine could attain such a grip as it did on the minds of Bible-reading people in spite of the theological claim prevalent among them that Jesus Christ is the highest revelation of God. One would think that they would immediately sense the clash between the two conceptions of God. A deity who could bear to curse innocent generations unborn of a particular ethnic or racial group is not the God revealed in the compassionate Galilean but is a sadistic and genocidal monster. Yet this is an example of the poisonous conclusions to which eisegesis can lead. We shall return to Genesis 9 later.

Not only did (and still do) White racists eisegete Genesis 9, but many of them drew heavily upon several passages attributed to the apostle Paul for their particular kind of biblical treatment. At this point it must suffice merely to list the passages and neither quote nor analyze them, for later in the chapter they will be briefly treated in an effort to give an example of the responsible and proper method of biblical interpretation. Some of the Pauline passages often used are 1 Corinthians 7:20-21; Ephesians 6:5-9 (many assumed Ephesians to be authored by Paul); Colossians 3:22-4:1; 1 Timothy 6:20-21; and Philemon vs. 10-18. Acts 17:26 was often included, for, although Acts is attributed to the pen of Luke, the passage is considered to be taken from one of Paul's addresses.

Of all the noted persons of the early church days, Paul appears to be the most vulnerable to eisegesis and misinterpretation. All that a fervent eisegeter has to do to misrepresent Paul's writings and thought is to ignore their historical context.

Paul's vulnerability to eisegesis and distortion is not due to anything heretical or anti-Christian in his thought but rather due to several other factors. For one thing, modern criticism of Paul is done over two thousands years of retrospective viewing, often without the critic's realization that Paul contributed to today's value vantage point. Without that element in the Christian faith which caused him to write the letter to Philemon there may not have been any abolitionists in New England or Quakers in Pennsylvania.

But aside from that factor making Paul vulnerable to criticism by those who dislike him and to eisegesis by those who would use him, there are other reasons for his being open to distortion. First, more of his writings or letters were preserved than those of any other early church notable. Secondly, Paul was no systematic theologian but a dedicated, busy, and practical exponent of the faith of the early church. He had neither the time nor the desire to measure a statement made in the present by one he had uttered in the past. Often the situation at hand dictated the solution to be applied at the moment, so long as the proposed remedy did not violate broad and unalterable Chrisitan principles (as in 1 Corinthians 7:25).

Another fact which is usually unknown to either Paul's critics or his distorters is that Paul had tremendous faith in the transforming power of the Christian faith. He felt that many of the major causes of human injustice and social friction would most assuredly be eliminated by Christ's being "all and in all," so that Christian believers would not need to dissipate their energies by taking potshots at symptoms. Being "in Christ" to Paul was the ultimate remedy.[4]

Yet the most ignored historical fact surrounding Paul's setting, and one without knowledge of which one cannot enter into a serious study of the apostle, is his intense and passionate conviction that the Second Coming or judgment day (Parousia) would dawn at any moment. In other words, he felt assured that the time span between the resurrection and the consummation was a very short one. Therefore much of the practical advice which he wrote to churches was of temporary value and designed just to tide the Christians over the few days left. Much of the fatherly instruction he offered on what under normal circumstances would have been routine matters, like marriage, divorce, and the work ethic, sounded strange under the Parousia's "interim ethic." In fact Paul came within a hair's breadth of discounting the need for slave uprisings (1 Corinthians 7:20-21) because he felt that the Parousia would make them unnecessary.

Ignoring all the above, the racist eisegetes, armed with the distorted interpretations of Genesis 9:18-27 and the Pauline passages cited, declared (some are still declaring) that the God of the Bible is the main author of Black innate inferiority and subservience. We shall return to these passages later.

Lest the reader at this point be inclined to feel that this writer has been expressing his imagination, let him note the testimony of some biblical and religious scholars regarding the biblical distortion alluded to. T. B. Maston has written:

> The curse of Canaan, frequently erroneously referred to as "the curse of Ham," was used in the past to justify slavery. It is being used by some people today to defend the *status quo* in race relations. They interpret the curse to mean that the Negro, as a descendant of Ham, is destined by God to fill permanently a subservient place in society, that he should never be considered as an equal by the white man. On the basis of the curse, some even contend that the Negro is innately inferior and that he can never lift

---

[4] *The Interpreter's One-Volume Commentary on the Bible,* Introduction to "The Letter of Paul to Philemon," by Victor Paul Furnish, pp. 894-895; see also *The New Oxford Annotated Bible* (New York: Oxford University Press, 1973), p. 1453.

himself or be lifted to the intellectual, cultural, or even moral level of other races.[5]

The late Kyle Haselden, a scholar and a true Southern gentleman, never ceased to confess vicariously for some of his fellow White churchmen the ungodly mind-set which placed Blacks on a low station. He wrote in his celebrated work: "Through the following years this contempt for the personality of the Negro had in every decade an official endorsement from some representative of the Christian Church, employing in the main Biblical arguments to prove the native inferiority of Negroes and their ordination as 'hewers of wood and drawers of water.'"[6]

George M. Fredrickson, who has obviously done considerable study in this area, pointed out how there was developed a link of cooperation and mutual support between the so-called scientific exponents of Black slavery and the notion of Black innate inferiority on the one hand and the advocates of the Ham doctrine on the other. Fredrickson states that not only did the country constantly wake up to the racist, sociological arguments of George Fitzhugh and the supporters of the "ethnological school," like Samuel A. Cartwright, Josiah C. Nott, and John H. Van Evrie, but also that, "The Biblical curse of Ham could serve almost as well, and in the hands of writers like Matthew Estes and Josiah Priest, it became a judgment of God which placed the black man virtually beyond the pale of humanity."[7]

It must be remembered, particularly now by Black people, that White racists were not eisegeting their favorite biblical passages solely for their own psychological comfort; they were feeding doses of these distorted interpretations to unlettered and helpless Blacks, young and old. There was method in their madness, so to speak. Carter G. Woodson, the granddaddy of Black church history, penned a sentence which spoke volumes in his effort to show how racist biblical interpretation had been imbedded in Black psyches working its brainwashing results. Woodson stated: "Literature especially

[5] T. B. Maston, *The Bible and Race* (Nashville: Broadman Press, 1959), p. 105. Used by permission.

[6] Kyle Haselden, *The Racial Problem in Christian Perspective* (New York: Harper & Row, Publishers, 1959), p. 51. See also George D. Kelsey, *Racism and the Christian Understanding of Man* (New York: Charles Scribner's Sons, 1965), pp. 104-113. Also H. Shelton Smith, *In His Image, but...* (Durham, N.C.: Duke University Press, 1972), pp. 130-131.

[7] George M. Fredrickson, *The Black Image in the White Mind* (New York: Harper & Row, Publishers, 1971), pp. 60-61.

adapted to this end prepared by churchmen safeguarding the interest of the slaveholding South was preferably used."[8]

More recently Gayraud Wilmore has reminded us of the mammoth effort to twist the Bible into an instrument for manipulating Black minds:

> The implications of "the freedom of the Christian man," basic to the New Testament and the theology of the Protestant Reformation, had no difficulty being recalled by the churches during the War of Independence. It was, however, assiduously avoided by most missionaries in their instruction to Negroes. Having convinced the dubious slaveowners that the conversion of his human property would not result in a capital loss, but greatly increase his profits, the missionary reduced Christian theology and ethics to their most simplistic and inoffensive affirmations. A favorite text was, of course, the passage from Ephesians 6:5—"Servants, be obedient to them that are your masters according to the flesh, with fear and trembling, in singleness of your heart, as unto Christ." By the middle of the nineteenth century several catechisms were available for oral instruction, such as Charles C. Jones's catechism for Presbyterian slaves and Capers' *"A Catechism for little Children and for Use on the Missions to the Slaves in South Carolina."* Most of these outlined the basic tenets of orthodoxy with suitable ethical injunctions calculated to inculcate the virtues of monogamy, honesty, industriousness, and to discourage the temptations to insurrections. One such document inquired of the slave: "What did God make you for?" The answer: "To make a crop." "What is the meaning of 'Thou shall not commit adultery'?" Answer: "To serve our heavenly Father, and our earthly master, obey our overseer, and not steal anything."[9]

We have now seen what happens when human creatures attempt to put words into the mouth of the divine Creator and Redeemer. Let us now turn to what transpires when God's Word is allowed to speak freely and for itself. In other words, let us view exegesis in its contrast to eisegesis.

When God Speaks for Himself—Exegesis

As in other branches of human knowledge and expertise, biblical scholars have their workable jargon or special terminology. They have a term associated with what most of them consider to be the proper procedure for rightly interpreting the Bible. That term is

---

[8] Carter G. Woodson, *The History of the Negro Church* (Washington, D.C.: The Associated Publishers, 1921), p. 165.
[9] Gayraud S. Wilmore, *Black Religion and Black Radicalism* (Garden City, N.Y.: Doubleday & Company, Inc., 1972), p. 34. Copyright © 1972 by Gayraud S. Wilmore. Reprinted by permission of Doubleday and Company.

exegesis. Like its opposite, eisegesis, it is taken also from the Greek. The Greek term from which it is taken is *ek* or *ech* meaning "out of" and *hegesthai,* lead. The functional idea here is that the real and genuine biblical message should be allowed to come "out of" the sacred writ in contrast to having some human preference imposed upon it or injected "into" it.

Exegesis and How İt Works

No responsible and effective Bible reading or interpretation can take place without diligent exegesis. It matters not how devotional, how pious, or how sincere one may be, he or she still will have to employ sound exegesis. This is not to say that personal devotion, faith, and commitment are not necessary to the understanding of and obedience to the biblical message. To the contrary, the biblical faith craves and demands one's total allegiance and involvement. But keep in mind that there are and have been many "sincere" people who have read their own notions, biases, and preferences "into" the Bible with disastrous results. "Little old ladies" in the missionary society believed the Ham doctrine years ago and swear by it now. Pastors and deacons at "gut level" believed in the past, and still do, that "God intended the races to be separate in all matters social," and that the Bible teaches that decree.

In other words, research must be coupled with piety. There must be a wedding of mind and heart. Reasoning from historical study must be teamed with the personal conviction stemming from rebirth by the Holy Spirit. One of the biggest tragedies of the American religious scene is the widespread notion that intelligence and reason are to be diligently applied to every area of human concern except religion. Even today in many religious and church circles the idea of biblical research is regarded as heresy and blasphemy. Persons urging biblical scholarship are charged with "tampering with the Bible." Yet serious Bible students should remember that in the Bible itself one is admonished to apply his or her mind as part of the totality of allegiance to God: "You must love the Lord your God with all your heart, with all your soul, with all your *mind,* and with all your strength" (Mark 12:30, TEV, italics added).

Therefore God does not intend for one to throw his or her mind out of gear, so to speak, when he or she comes to matters of faith, morals, and biblical interpretation. Exegesis based on research is a must as the proper approach to biblical interpretation. And as painful as it may be, the quasi-magical idea of biblical interpretation must be thrown out of the window. The magical concept is that, at all points and all times, all one has to do is to pray, pick up the Bible and read, and the Holy Spirit will immediately reveal the true meaning to the mind of the reader. This is just not true. It is a fact that with some more familiar passages in the Bible all that is necessary is a rereading within a devotional atmosphere. But even here, more often than not, one makes use rather unconsciously of one's own research or that which someone else has done. Exegesis is indispensable.

Then what is exegesis in terms of its structure and procedure? What are its steps, its building blocks? Biblical scholars have constantly reminded us that any responsible effort at biblical interpretation must attempt to find out what a passage or book of the Bible "meant" when it was first written before a statement is made as to what it "means" (today's application). In other words, the effort must be spent to cut through the thicket of years of obscurity and misinterpretation until the intent of its author and the understanding of its first readers can be determined. For example, to understand and appreciate Second Thessalonians, one has to know through the benefit of research that some Thessalonian Christians had become morbidly obsessed with the Second Coming of Jesus Christ, for today's reader was not there when the problem prompted Paul to write.

What are the steps in doing this necessary spadework? The serious researcher must make use of scholars in the area of biblical research. He or she should read diligently what is written in the field but should also keep in mind that not everything written rests on sound scholarship and that not everything said in a lecture or a sermon has God's approval. Spend as much time as possible determining which "reputable" scholars are to be read and heard.

Then from the output of such reputable scholars (who may be authors of notable works, seminary professors, trained pastors, college teachers, and dedicated lay churchworkers) find out the "setting" of the biblical book or passage. The setting has two aspects—the literary context and the historical context.

The "literary context" is a phrase which reminds us: (1) that the whole passage must be read and kept in mind so that one is not trapped into reading just a part of it; (2) that knowledge of certain words, terms, phrases, sentences, and metaphors coming from ancient languages and past centuries is important; and (3) that for us to understand such literary aspects, we must rely to a great extent on persons who have studied the ancient documents and archeological findings which throw light on the Bible today. The literary context of a passage must be known by the reader in order that full understanding of that passage may be enjoyed.

The historical context, as the wording implies, represents the thrust which seeks out the historical facts surrounding a book or passage in the Bible. Through research, the answers to the following historical questions must be answered—or as many of them as possible. Who wrote the book? When was it written? To whom was it written? Where was it written? What was the problem or purpose which prompted the writing? What constitutes the political, economic, social, and religious background of the period and area? Once the researcher has dug out the answers to the above questions, he or she is well on the way to honestly saying not only what the book or passage meant two or three millennia ago but also what it means as applied to the human situation now. But, without this necessary historical tunneling, eisegesis is sure to rush in and fill the void.

Along with the exegetical approach just described, the serious Bible student must carry another fact to biblical research. Regardless of what images, symbols, parables, models, allegories, faith portraits,* or descriptions were used by those prescientific-minded biblical authors, their central concern as well as the central concern of the Bible as a whole was the "God-man relationship" or the "divine-human encounter." Our scientific categories were unknown to them just as ours will appear alien to people centuries from now. Our categorical distinctions, such as separating "biology" from "theology," just were unheard of in their day. But the realities they pointed out in their time making for good and for ill are just as evident and potent for us today. "Demons" of hatred, fear, bigotry, distrust, and illness still plague human beings today and must be "cast out." Greed, lust for power, immorality, and murder can still be found in the human family. Radical reorientation (rebirth) is still needed to change and heal warped souls and tainted hearts.

Therefore, the bibical writers, regardless of what categories of explanation they drew upon to say it, believed that "in the beginning, God . . ." and "in the end, God," and that we are God's special creation and co-creators with him. One needs not worry about attempting to square the early poetic chapters of Genesis with modern geological, zoological, and biological findings, for the author was more concerned about his affirmation that all came from God than he was about his statement of how it came. So when reading the Bible, just remember the central concern is the point when and where God and the person meet or, in other words: Where is man or woman in relation to God? "And the Lord God called unto Adam, and said unto him, Where art thou?" (Genesis 3:9, KJV).

Diligent exegesis and the recognition that the main biblical concern is not biology, zoology, or geology but divine-human encounter constitute the two tools of proper biblical interpretation. The biblical God who is active Creator, Redeemer, and Liberator calls his people, particularly the oppressed, into active response to his liberating activity. This is the essence of the divine-human encounter. The employment of exegesis and the recognition that divine-human encounter is the main concern of sacred writ is what some have referred to as the historical-theological method of interpreting the Bible.

Examples of Responsible Biblical Interpretation

In order to give an example of exegesis, let us briefly examine the racists' pet passages, keeping in mind that these biblical quotations have been and are used to support the kinds of notions, theories, and convictions undergirding Black enslavement, claims of Black innate inferiority, the segregation of and the discrimination against Blacks by Whites using race as a basis. The passage on which the Ham doctrine is based is Genesis 9:18-27. The Pauline passages used are Ephesians 6:5-9 (many assumed Ephesians to be Pauline); Colossians 3:22-4:1; 1 Timothy 6:20-21; and Philemon, verses 10-18. In Acts 17:22-31 the address to the council of Areopagus is attributed to Paul, although Luke wrote the Acts of the Apostles. (Note that racist eisegetes often found useful the latter part of verse 26 about keeping within one's boundaries.)

The sacred legend of Genesis 9:18-27 relates that after the great flood Noah and his three sons, Shem, Ham, and Japheth, emerged from the ark and established residence. Noah became a grower of fruit from the vines. Once he became intoxicated from the wine he made, and while he was lying in a drunken stupor, his son Ham (or Canaan?) made sport of him. Noah's other two sons shielded him from further disgrace and informed him of what Ham had done. It is reported that when Noah awoke, he pronounced this curse upon Ham (Canaan):

"Cursed be Canaan;
   a slave of slaves shall he be to his brothers." . . .
"Blessed by the Lord my God be Shem;
   and let Canaan be his slave.
God enlarge Japheth,
   and let him dwell in the tents of Shem;
   and let Canaan be his slave" (Genesis 9:25-27).

This is the passage into which racist eisegetes read a divine curse universally and for all time visited upon Blacks. But what is revealed about it under thorough exegesis? Who wrote Genesis? Genesis was written not by one author but by several. It is composed of several documents woven together. When was it written? Parts of it were written at various times dating from the middle of the eighth century B.C. to 539 B.C. There are few reputable scholars who will promise to give the exact date when the strands were woven together. Where was it written? It was written (that is the documents woven together) somewhere in the Israelite tribal territories. As to its recipients and its purpose, the various narratives were put together as a sacred faith saga * for all Israelites who cared about their heritage, history, and destiny under the creative, redemptive, and liberating God of their fathers.

This saga had to answer questions which rested heavily upon the minds of the ancient Israelites who like their modern counterparts looked for meaning in their existence. But, unlike their modern counterparts, the early ancients recited their meaning in story form long before they learned to write it. Their social, political, economic, and religious experience was "told" in order to grasp life's meaning. They answered in simple story form such questions as these: Why do human beings go to war against other human beings? How did evil get into a good creation by a good God? How did different languages come about? How did the earth come to be? What is the origin of natural disasters, such as floods and volcanic eruptions (fire and brimstone from heaven)?

But, perhaps most of all, the Israelites themselves had to have an answer to why nations and tribes with obviously similar characteristics became historical enemies who seemingly could never reconcile their differences and curb their hostilities toward one another. The hostility between the Israelites and the Canaanites * is an example. The Israelites perhaps needed an answer to the question which grew out of that long conflict.

Yet the sacred saga could be reaching for something primal which goes beyond answers to historical conflict and touches the basic difference between Israelite and Canaanite religions, the difference between the ethical and prophetic Yahwism on the one hand and the agricultural, individualist, and quasi-magical religion of Canaan on the other hand. Perhaps deep in their historical mind-set the Israelites regretted leaving the nomadic, pastoral life in which they could march with God and support their neighbor and settling down in the greed, strife, and competition of the agricultural life where Baal was ruler.

Note the footnote in the *New Oxford Annotated Bible* on this point: "Since the curse was later put on Canaan rather than Ham (v. 26), it is likely that Canaan was the actor originally. **24:** Here Noah's *youngest son* is clearly Canaan, not Ham as in v. 22. **25:** The curse implies that Canaan's subjugation to Israel was the result of Canaanite sexual perversions (Lev. 18:24-30)." [10]

It should now be clear that the authors of the book of Genesis in general and the author of Genesis 9:18-27 in particular had no racial or color distinction in mind at all. Nowhere does it say in the Bible that Ham or Canaan is the father of Black people. In fact, when the Bible mentions Blacks, it employs the terms "Ethiopian" and "Nubian." The Canaanite was not regarded as being Black.

To top it off, this sacred legend or saga is most likely not historical at all. It may have to take its place with legends, like the Flood and the tower of Babel, as being of theological and aetiological * value but nonhistorical. Therefore, it was only the racists' ego need that caused them to read racism into the passage. Perhaps the world would have been better off if such persons had read the passage with a comical eye like T. B. Maston who not only pointed out that certain psalms refer to Egypt as the land of Ham (Psalm 78:51; Psalm 105:23, 26-27; Psalm 106:21-22) but also raised the rib-tickling thought that nowhere does it say that God agreed with the curse which Noah pronounced. [11]

When exegesis is brought to bear upon the Pauline passage, the racists' eisegetical case is almost thrown out of court from the start by the fact that much of Paul's practical (as opposed to theological advice) exhortation is composed of interim ethics in anticipation of a very early Second Coming. There are many who have not exercised

[10] *The New Oxford Annotated Bible,* pp. 11-12.
[11] Maston, *op. cit.,* pp. 112-113.

the balanced scholarship of separating Paul's solid theology ("I have received from the Lord . . .") from his practical, interim advice (1 Corinthians 7:6, 12, 20, 25-35). Paul himself would be the first to caution us against making theological absolutes out of his interim advice.

Yet, when forced out of context, some of the passages do leave some doubt in the minds of some who would refute White racism. One thing can be said from the outset. Neither passage was originally intended by its authors to condone human slavery as a structure instituted and sanctioned by God.

Let us take Ephesians 6:5-9 under exegesis. The claim that Paul was the author of Ephesians is not too well regarded today. Yet this does not make the letter or work less Christian or useful. Some scholars are uncertain about the date, and speculation has it ranging from A.D. 62 to A.D. 95. It is clear that it was written to Asian Christians, predominantly Greek in composition. If Paul wrote it, it was written from a Roman jail. If he did not, anywhere in Asia Minor could have been its place of writing. While practical purpose or problems prompted most of the Pauline letters (Romans seems to be an exception), Ephesians seems to have been written for general reading by the whole region.

The general purpose is to persuade the Christian coming under the influence of the letter to take a reverent retrospective (a look back) glance at the great Christian past with its faithful models and martyrs and thereby sense God's grand design of reconciling all things in the universe to himself through Jesus Christ. The background is most likely that the Gentile (non-Jewish) congregations have drifted away from early Jewish church heritage which revered the apostles and martyred deacons of the early church.

Ephesians 6:5-9 reads:

> Slaves, be obedient to those who are your earthly masters, with fear and trembling, in singleness of heart, as to Christ; *not in the way of eye-service, as men-pleasers, but as servants of Christ,* doing the will of God from the heart, rendering service with a *good will as to the Lord and not to men,* knowing that whatever good any one does, he will receive the same again from the Lord, whether he is a slave or free. Masters, do the same to them and *forbear threatening, knowing that he who is both their Master and yours is in heaven, and that there is no partiality* with him.

The emphasis is mine to point up something quite phenomenal when one realizes that the Christian movement found the institution of human slavery already present and perfectly legal. The amazing thing is the strong language to the slave owner and the slave. In the language to the slave owner, the jagged edge of contempt sticks out even to the point of being threatening. In effect it says that God cares no more for the slave owner than he does for the slave and He can show this concern at any point.

Because this passage deals with the existing situation of slavery, it has been a buttress of the arguments of the racist eisegetes. Even so, as Gayraud Wilmore has suggested, it is in reality a clue to the beginning of the Christian movement's erosion of the institution of human slavery.

Note that it was mentioned earlier that the theme and purpose of Ephesians attempted to show that God's "grand design," as Maxie S. Gordon likes to call it, is to reconcile "all things" unto himself through Christ. Then "all things" would have to include conflicts in human relations caused by "big I's and little you's." The author himself states that the status thing that human beings have here on earth is not in God. God is no respecter of persons.

In other words, the author is saying that in God's reconciling process all relationships and allegiances are geared to a higher realm, beyond the pleasing of men, beyond threats and intimidations and the fear of them. Thus, the exegesis of this passage which at first appeared in some degree to support human slavery shows that the opposite is the case. For when one's allegiance is lifted from a human owner to Christ, one cannot abide a slave master. In God's reconciling plan, masters would not be masters in the old sense of the case and slaves would not be slaves in the old sense. The old structures, mind-sets, categories, power levers, and value systems will be done away.

Colossians 3:22–4:1 is similar to the Ephesians passage in background, theme, and purpose. It is further similar in exhortation. Some scholars who do not attribute Pauline authorship to Ephesians claim that the author of Ephesians may have copied from Colossians.

Colossians was written by Paul sometime between A.D. 60 and 62 from Rome to the Colossian Christians. It was written to furnish strength to the church membership and a rebuttal against a group of cosmic philosophers and angel worshipers at the same time. This cosmic group in its door-to-door and church-to-church activity had been teaching that Jesus Christ was only "one" of the sacred or cosmic beings in a whole hierarchy to be placated and attained until all the steps of the ladder were achieved by the talented few who had the right formula. Paul responded by pointing out that Jesus Christ is *the* God appointed mediator and reconciler who makes all other mediation unnecessary. In Christ dwells God in all his fullness.

The passage is almost word for word as that in Ephesians. But in reading Colossians 3:22–4:1 under exegesis, one feels Paul's sense of pressure of his conviction of the Second Coming. The reward will be here soon (3:24). "Walk in wisdom toward them that are without, redeeming the time" (4:5, KJV). The "time" is short, as far as Paul is concerned, when Christ will return and rectify all structures, relationships, and worlds.

Perhaps with the exceptions of First and Second Thessalonians, Paul's belief in an early Second Coming shows up nowhere more than in 1 Corinthians 7. It is therefore interesting to note that 7:20-21 eisegeted so much by racists boomerangs on them. The passage reads: "Every one should remain in the state in which he was called. Were you a slave when called? Never mind. But if you can gain your freedom, avail yourself of the opportunity." In other words, here even a casual reading of the literary context proves just the opposite of the racists' contention that Paul condoned slavery in the name of God. What the passage shows is that in spite of Paul's advice that for the short time remaining Christians ought to suspend or freeze all general plans, he found the achievement of human freedom important enough to be made an exception to the interim ethic. Read the passage in its context again. Circumcision, marriage, divorce, funerals, fun, and business deals can all be "put off." But it is not so with freedom activities. Paul almost included it in the list of concerns to be suspended. Yet he catches himself: "Well, never mind; but if you do have a chance to become a free man, use it" (TEV).

Exegesis indeed shows that the expectation of an early Second Coming greatly influenced Paul as he wrote First Corinthians (7:29-31) sometime around A.D. 54 from Ephesus. Everyone and everything eventually met in this crossroads city. Much that came never left.

The church at Corinth reflected this clash of persons, ideas, ideals, and practices and possessed more than its share of problems. Many of the new converts had come from the emotional and wild mystery religions given to frenzy and lusty parties.

Many of the problems were referred to Paul, their spiritual leader, for solutions. The problems consisted of cliques in the church, immoral sexual behavior, legal scandals among church members, the dispute over women's decorum and dress particularly in church, the dispute over priorities in the present situation touching marriage and other ordinarily routine matters, the distortion of the Lord's Supper, and the disruptive practice of babbling in "unknown tongues" obviously brought over from the mystery religion cults. The Corinthian church had not one but many problems.

Rest assured that Paul's mind was far from creating a justification of human slavery. Jesus Christ, according to Paul's conviction, would return any day with a brand-new order of things. But, as has already been stated, if one wishes to isolate 1 Corinthians 7:20-21 in spite of what its historical context shows (Paul's strong conviction of an early Second Coming), one will soon see that the literary context shows that Paul even refused to include human slavery in the list of things to be tolerated even for a brief period.

As far as Acts 17:26 and 1 Timothy 6:20-21 are concerned, little time is required to sense that racist eisegetes grievously wrenched both out of context. Instead of advocating racial or ethnic segregation, Paul is reported by Luke (the author of Acts around A.D. 90), Paul's close companion, as advocating the oneness of the human race in Acts 17:26, drawing upon Stoic poets. If Paul believed in the separation of different groups and races, as segregationists have maintained, what was he, a Jew, doing in Athens? Obviously he was there because he truly believed that "From the one man he created all races of men, and made them live over the whole earth" (TEV).

The claim that 1 Timothy 6:20-21 forbids any criticism of the system of racial segregation should not even be honored with an answer. Yet necessity sometimes comes to us in the fact that there are still a few persons whose not knowing makes them vulnerable to the wildest claims. There are times when it is risky to assume that all are knowledgeable when it comes to the Bible. The passage reads: "O Timothy, guard what has been entrusted to you. Avoid the godless chatter and contradictions of what is falsely called knowledge, for by professing it some have missed the mark as regards the faith."

Even as late as the Civil Rights Movement of the late fifties and sixties, segregationists used this passage as a proof-text against persons who would "tamper" with the social system which, according to them, was ordained by God to remain forever segregated. Anyone, they maintained, who teaches or advocates otherwise is violating God's word by the use of "vain knowledge and contradictions."

The truth of the matter is that the author of First Timothy (whether

Paul or someone else), writing some time between A.D. 90 and 115, was faced with an onslaught of false teaching and alien doctrines which threatened to do injury to the church. Scholars tell us that the heretical belief-system consisted of a mixture of gnosticism (which denied the essential goodness of creation and the genuineness of the incarnation) on the one hand and on the other, Persian dualism (which claimed that good and evil would coexist forever, neither ever overcoming the other because the two "contradictions" needed each other). This epistle like the other pastoral letter has nothing to do with ethnic or racial segregation. Rather, they were written to help preserve the core of the church's convictions: God is *Creator, Redeemer, and Liberator among us, who will ultimately destroy Satan (all evil) and reign forever.* It is blasphemous and absurd to read into this noble tract the poison of bigotry.

We now come to Paul's letter to Philemon and the Colossian church which many racists have relied upon as final and positive proof that Paul agreed with human slavery. Their main contention is that the fact that Paul sent the runaway slave, Onesimus, back to his master shows beyond the shadow of a doubt that Paul regarded the system of slavery as divinely sanctioned.

It has been wisely said that there is no end to the contradictions which Satan spins in the minds of those whom he controls. The cold, irrefutable truth is that Philemon is the one production from Paul's pen which clearly reveals what Paul personally felt about the odious yet legalized system of human slavery in the ancient world. The letter is short enough and its purpose, background, and destination clear enough that the full impact of what was happening can be felt.

The historical-theological background of Philemon, verses 10-18, is this: While the apostle Paul was in Rome awaiting the results of his appeal of his conviction to the emperor, a young, runaway slave who had been listening to some of Paul's messages became converted and during counseling confessed to Paul that he was a fugitive from justice. It so happened that his slave-master was Philemon, a noted and respected deacon of the church at Colossae.

Both Onesimus, the slave, and Paul in session decided that the safest alternative for the new convert would be a return to his master, although he would not be able to make restitution for the material he stole prior to his flight. But Paul was determined that Onesimus would return with a new status behind which he, the apostle, would squarely stand.

Paul sent his personal companion with his new "son in Christ" bearing a letter to Philemon to be read to the whole church. This is part of the letter:

So I make a request to you *on behalf of Onesimus,* who is my own son in Christ; for while in prison I have become his spiritual father. At one time he was of no use to you, but now he is useful both to you and to me.

I am sending him back to you now, *and with him goes my heart.* I would like to keep him here with me, while I am in prison for the gospel's sake, so that he could help me in your place. However, I do not want to force you to help me; rather, I would like for you to do it of your own free will. So I will not do a thing unless you agree.

It may be that Onesimus was away from you for a short time so that you might have him back for all time. And now he is not just a slave, *but much more than a slave: he is a dear brother in Christ.* How much he means to me! And how much more he will mean to you, both as a slave and as a brother in the Lord!

So, if you think of me as your partner, welcome him back just as you would welcome me. If he has done you any wrong, or owes you anything, charge it to my account (vv. 10-18, TEV, italics mine).

These hardly seem to be the words of a person who views human slavery as being compatible with and ordained by the gospel of Jesus Christ as so many proslavery and segregationist church members have contended. In spite of the legality slavery enjoyed and in spite of Paul's conviction of an early return of Christ, this letter (note the italics) reveals a man who saw the irreconcilable friction between the gospel and human slavery. To those who from the twentieth-century vantage point brand Paul as either a pro-slaver or a coward, let it be said that if early American planters and legislators had been one-third as honest, human, and sensitive as the apostle, we would not be facing the results of the "fatal dichotomy." When the question "Did conversion set a Black slave free?" was asked, the final answer was, "No, his inward status had nothing to do with his outward status." This pernicious and fatal dichotomy undid the work of the Reformation. That dichotomy set off a chain of dichotomies— separation between secular and sacred, between soul and body, between religion and life, and between White and Black.

The conclusion ought to be clear that the passages cited by racist eisegetes as providing divine sanction for Black slavery and Black innate inferiority leave such proof lacking when viewed under research. In all cases cited, the authors themselves were not laboring under any sort of race theories. Biblical writers knew no race theories in the sense that we know them today. Color prejudice is a late phenomenon. Few if any ancient peoples ever enslaved human beings on the basis of color. An ancient nation enslaved whomever it conquered, regardless of color. Therefore, let no one run to the Bible to prove the superiority or inferiority of a people of any color or racial or ethnic origin. The historic result of such efforts on the part of White racists has been to cause many Blacks to feel that American racism and American Christianity are of one piece. This is what James H. Cone was expressing when he wrote: "Naturally, as the slave questions his existence as a slave, he also questions the religion of the enslaver." [12]

What Is Biblical Revelation?

Any serious Bible student will be at a severe loss without a clear understanding of how and in what sense God reveals himself in and through the Bible. What constitutes biblical revelation, and what does it clarify about the nature of God?

Here three things must honestly be said. The first is that men wrote the various documents and letters which are collectively called the Bible. God inspired the writing of the Bible, but men wrote it. These writers were not cast into some sort of trance or coma when they wrote. They were not entranced persons; they were transformed persons. God does not impersonally "use" human beings to do his will. He transforms them by the Holy Spirit so that they then voluntarily and actively choose to do his will of redemption and liberation.

The second thing to be said is that the Bible contains the "word" and not "words" of God. The singular term "word" should be thought of by the Bible reader as fairly synonymous with terms like "communication" or "clarification" or "message." The Bible reader should not get "hung up" on the wild idea that God has some pet language or a "special" set of sacred words or phrases to be chanted or repeated. God's truth, mandates, and activities can be expressed in any language, for he is a God who acts, and for him "word" always must be "made flesh." Through the biblical events, divine-human encounters, human models, and primarily God's chief revelatory person, Jesus, the "Word made flesh," God communes with and communicates to men and women.

[12] James H. Cone, *Black Theology and Black Power* (New York: The Seabury Press, Inc., 1969). p. 33, copyright © 1969 by The Seabury Press, Inc. Used by permission of the publisher.

The third matter for the Bible student to remember is that in and through the Bible God primarily gives and reveals himself to us, and only secondarily does he give information "about" himself. This divine self-giving and presence is always in the form of power and direction in active cooperation with a people ready to respond actively in kind.

For verily the God revealed in the Bible is more a *verb* than a noun. He reveals himself through his acts, through what he causes to happen (Exodus 3:14), liberating and redeeming actions. One should never ask, "Have you seen God?" but rather, "Are you witnessing and cooperating with what God is doing?" For it is in his acts that God is truly known.

This understanding of the nature of God is the reason that the Bible and what it reveals are powerfully relevant to Black liberation activity today. The biblical God's active presence and power for liberation calls for, nay demands, the active response of all who would be free and whole, who would reach God's "Promised Land." [13]

In the live Black communities today, Black liberation must be the subject, predicate, and the object. All efforts must be funneled into the rediscovery of the outlines of the Black past and the present shaping of the kinds of strategies and methodologies to determine Black goals and destinies. And the Black communities should adopt "their" answers instead of hand-me-down directions. Black questions should receive Black answers which have been filtered through, tested in, and sanctified by the experiences of the people who asked them.

A great part of that Black, sanctifying experience was shaped and hallowed by the Black American religious faith informed and undergirded by the Bible. For in the Bible are events, models, persons, stories, and insights growing out of the history and experiences of oppressed people both in the Old Testament and the New Testament. Let us now view this history with Black eyes.

Questions for Further Study

1. What are some safeguards against reading personal biases into Scripture today?

[13] To this writer, the terms "freedom," "wholeness," and "Promised Land" are not verbal supports for empty rhetoric but can be readily defined. "Freedom and wholeness" mean that condition bereft of any human powers, structures, systems, strategies, or procedures which arbitrarily and unjustly interfere with the full exercise of a human being's potentialities and urges for health. "Promised Land" means similarly what the Founding Fathers meant by the political model "unalienable rights" and what the biblical model in Luke 4:16-21 conveys.

2. What evidence is there that past efforts to give biblical sanction to human slavery and racial segregation in America were deliberate?
3. In what ways are contemporary efforts to revive and give academic respectability to the Black-White comparative genes arguments secular versions of the old Ham doctrine?
4. How did American Bible reading become perverted by the preoccupation with the attempt to justify the institution of slavery?
5. What are some necessary steps that Black churches should take to train their church school teachers in biblical understanding?
6. In what ways, if any, has the apostle Paul been erroneously interpreted?

Additional Reading

Fredrickson, George M., *The Black Image in the White Mind.* New York: Harper & Row, Publishers, 1971.

Haselden, Kyle, *The Racial Problem in Christian Perspective.* New York: Harper & Row, Publishers, 1959.

Kelsey, George, *Racism and the Christian Understanding of Man.* New York: Charles Scribner's Sons, 1965.

Maston, T. B., *The Bible and Race.* Nashville: Broadman Press, 1959.

Smith. H. Shelton, *In His Image, but: Racism in Southern Religion, 1780-1910.* Durham, N.C.: Duke University Press, 1972.

Stampp, Kenneth M., "To Make Them Stand in Fear," *The Black Church in America,* Hart M. Nelsen, *et. al.,* eds. New York: Basic Books, 1971.

Wilmore, Gayraud, *Black Religion and Black Radicalism.* Garden City, N.Y.: Doubleday & Company, Inc., 1972.

The Old Testament and the Black American

In Eastern Arabia several millennia ago, not too far from where Asia and Africa join, a pastoral-nomadic tribe of Semitic stock went on the move. Its main point of identity was its internal group loyalty and a conviction by its elders that the group was being pulled, directed, and protected by the Sovereign Power of all human destiny. This group wandered around between Asia and North Africa in hardship and adversity, and the clan evolved into several tribes which required the expansion of their loyalties and their understanding of their destiny, which to them came to be interpreted as being a model to other nations relative to integrity and social harmony.

These tribes were eventually given a land grant by an Egyptian dynasty, but after a change in the ruling administration in Egypt, the tribes were forced into slave labor. After several centuries, the tribes rebelled and escaped under the guidance of rebel leaders, wandered for a time in the desert, and then formed a confederacy* in Palestine centered upon a religious interpretation of their destiny and past experience. They believed that the hardships they had endured, the narrow escapes, and liberating experiences they could talk about did not come about by ordinary effort. They attributed these to their God

45

and promised to be totally loyal to him by periodically acknowledging his presence and by always treating one another with justice, compassion, and humility that other nations would be able to pattern after them.

The tribes were eventually shaped into a nation which reached a peak of wealth, power, and prominence. But at every point in the history of the confederacy and the nation when social injustice or religious disloyalty was detected, persons who served as the conscience of the people would remind them of the promise of total loyalty and ethical zeal they made to the God who had rescued and guided them and was still doing the same as their friend. But as in many nations, concern for the promise to the God of their destiny faded. The nation decayed and was again enslaved.

But even then there were among them spokesmen who assured them that their God would revive them and still make them his instrument of his plan to redeem the earth. That nation never regained the prominence earlier known, but from its people came persons who have figured significantly in the redemption of the earth and who have reminded the world that God is still at work liberating and redeeming those who will obey him.

This, then, is the story of Israel. In its experience of bitterness and glory, slackness and obedience, despair and hope, there are models for people in a similar existence. Black people are experiencing such an existence.

Black Experience and the Old Testament

The parallel or comparison between the experience of ancient Israelites and Black Americans forces itself upon the mind of even the casual observer. The comparison between the two experiences is not clear-cut and identical at all points, to be sure. For each people's experience is uniquely its own and self-validating. However, both the Israelite experience and the Black American experience reveal a people who, beyond their share, suffered consequences not self-imposed, who in seeking liberation and meaning looked to God for an interpretation of their peoplehood, task, and destiny. Robert A. Bennett writes:

> The Black experience in America is not the Jewish-Christian experience in ancient Palestine. But as the tale of sorrows of a people awaiting deliverance, the black narrative has a message consistent with the biblical witness though not to be found in that witness. It is a testimony of its own,

distinct from Scripture even as it would proclaim its word to us in biblical images and in the categories of scriptural revelation.[1]

The Israelite experience as reflected in the Old Testament is that a people, often fragmented and oppressed and always exposed to all the risks and dangers of life, felt themselves called by God to fulfill a certain destiny. They made a covenant * (a two-way agreement) with God based on what God had done, was doing, and would do for them. In that covenant the people understood that God had already given a clue to what he would continue to do for them by what he had already done: namely, liberate and direct them forever toward their destiny. The people understood their side of the agreement to be total loyalty and obedience to God and high ethical living characterized by justice, compassion, and humility in human relations.

Now the parallel between the Israelite covenantal experience and the Black American experience is easy to see. As for the Black Americans, here are a people, uprooted, fragmented, and enslaved in the early days, oppressed and held down to this day, who have looked to God for some interpretation of and full liberation from their misery. They also look for clues to their destiny, feeling that in God there must be some purpose in all this trouble, either because of it or in spite of it. Later on, many American Blacks became convinced that God was in this painful and oppressive situation with them helping them survive, endure, and increase in numbers in spite of the efforts of those who held power over them. There are today Blacks in this country who not only see the active hand of God in Black survival but also see as God's action the events and forces which have made for more recent Black gains in the areas of civil, social, economic, and political rights. One Black churchwoman was heard to cry out in a church service: "Dear Jesus! The white bigot said never, but my God said forever! You know my God is Alpha and Omega!" She no doubt was thinking of school desegregation.

Therefore, the parallel and empathetic link between the experience of the two peoples are that two suffering, fragmented, and oppressed peoples felt themselves being delivered, shaped, called, and directed by God toward a God-given destiny. And for the American Black people, the miracle of it all is that they sensed this parallel when they read the Bible. Note that, in spite of the efforts already cited of White

[1] Robert A. Bennett, "Black Experience and the Bible," Martin E. Marty and Dean G. Peerman, editors, *New Theology No. 9* (New York: The Macmillan Company, 1962), pp. 177-178. Reprinted by permission of *Theology Today*.

racists to eisegete and dilute the biblical message so as to brainwash
Blacks, there were many Blacks in the early days of the country who
understood the real biblical faith. The Black scholar, Gayraud S.
Wilmore, emphasized this fact in chapters 2 and 3 of his very
thorough work.[2]

As an example of how some Black "militants" even in the days of
slavery interpreted the Bible with emphasis on the Old Testament, let
us note some excerpts from "David Walker's Appeal," noting how
Walker makes use of biblical categories, images, and symbols.[3]

Directing his message to white oppressors he wrote:

> . . . I say, the Americans want us, the property of the Holy Ghost, to serve
> them. But there is a day fast approaching, when (unless there is a universal
> repentance [a] on the part of the whites, which will scarcely take place, they
> have got to be so hardened in consequence of our blood, and so wise in
> their own conceit). [b] To be plain and candid with you, Americans! I say
> that the day is fast approaching, when there will be a greater time on the
> continent of America, than ever was witnessed upon this earth, since it
> came from the hand of its Creator. [c] Some of you have done us so much
> injury, that you will never be able to repent.—Your cup must be filled.—
> You want us for your slaves, and shall have enough of us—God is just, *who
> will give your fill of us. . . .* [d]

In another place he wrote:

> . . . I have several times called the white Americans our *natural enemies*—I
> shall here define my meaning of the phrase. Shem, Ham and Japheth,
> together with their father Noah [e] and wives, I believe were not natural
> enemies to each other. When the ark rested after the flood upon Mount
> Ararat, in Asia, they (eight) were all the people which could be found alive
> in all the earth—in fact if Scriptures be true (which I believe are) there were
> no other living men in all the earth, notwithstanding some ignorant
> creatures hesitate not to tell us that we (the blacks) are the seed of Cain the
> murderer of his brother Abel. [f] But where or of whom those ignorant and
> avaricious wretches could have gotten their information, I am unable to
> declare. Did they receive it from the Bible? I have searched the Bible as well

[2] Gayraud S. Wilmore, *Black Religion and Black Radicalism* (Garden City, N.Y.:
Doubleday & Company, Inc., 1972).
[3] Note: The locations of biblical images and symbols which, in the writer's judgment,
Walker drew upon are listed for the reader who wishes to read them on his/her own.
They are indicated by italic letters. It would be too cumbersome to quote all of the
biblical passages noted.
[a] Isaiah 1:10-20; Jeremiah 8:6; Acts 8:18-22; Mark 1:15—all carry the theme.
[b] Proverbs 26:5.
[c] Genesis 1:1.
[d] Romans 3:25-26.
[e] Genesis 6:8-10-1.
[f] Genesis 4:1-16.

as they, if I am not as well learned as they are, and have never seen a verse which testifies whether we are the seed of Cain or of Abel. Yet those men tell us that we are the seed of Cain, and that God put a dark stain upon us, that we might be known as their slaves!!! Now, I ask those avaricious and ignorant wretches, who act more like the seed of Cain, by murdering [,] the whites or the blacks? How many vessel loads of human beings have the blacks thrown into the seas? How many thousand souls have the blacks murdered in cold blood, to make them work in wretchedness and ignorance, to support them and their families?

And further on, Walker pens:

Man is a peculiar creature—he is the image of his God, g though he may be subjected to the most wretched condition upon earth, yet the spirit and feeling which constitute the creature, man, can never be entirely erased from his breast, because the God who made him after his own image, planted it in his heart; he cannot get rid of it. The whites knowing this, they do not know what to do; they know that they have done us so much injury, they are afraid that we, being men, and not brutes, will retaliate, and woe will be to them; therefore, that dreadful fear, together with an avaricious spirit, and the natural love in them, to be called masters (which term will yet honour them with to their sorrow) bring them to the resolve that they will keep us in ignorance and wretchedness, as long as they possibly can, and make the best of their time, while it lasts. Consequently, they, themselves, (and not us) render themselves our natural enemies, by treating us so cruel. They keep us miserable now, and call us their property, but some of them will have enough of us by and by—their stomachs shall run over with us; they want us for their slaves, and shall have us to their fill. We are all in the world together!! h —I said above, because we cannot help ourselves, (viz. we cannot help the whites murdering our mothers and our wives) but this statement is incorrect—for we can help ourselves; for, if we lay aside abject servility, and be determined to act like men, and not brutes—the murderers among the whites would be afraid to show their cruel heads.[4]

The case of David Walker, the militant Bible reader, was not an isolated exception. There were other Blacks who concluded with the same interpretation. Gabriel Prosser and Nat Turner of Virginia were brush-arbor preachers. Denmark Vessey of South Carolina was a deacon. Sojourner Truth and Harriet Tubman quoted Scripture to back up what they were doing in the service of the Underground Railroad. Frederick Douglass often based his sense of human justice upon the Bible. However, the towering freedom names of the past

g Genesis 1:26-27.
h The point made by the apostle Paul in Acts 17:26-27.
[4] David Walker, "David Walker's Appeal," *Black Protest,* ed. Joanne Grant (Greenwich, Conn.: Fawcett Publications, Inc., 1968), pp. 84-87.

should not be regarded as giving the impression that the grassroots Blacks who read and heard read the Bible were all gullible, docile, cowardly and easygoing. Black members in predominantly White congregations in the North separated themselves in the early days of the country. In the South where in many areas there were laws against Blacks' coming together in groups, Black church members met in secret, read the Bible, preached sermons, and sang freedom code hymns.

These were the people who saw themselves in the Bible, so to speak. These were those who saw Israel's God of liberation, social justice, and redemption as their God because in some real sense they saw themselves as God's Israel in their own time preparing to escape Pharaoh's bondage and to possess the Promised Land. They identified themselves with Shadrach, Meshach, and Abednego in the fiery furnace, with Daniel in the lion's den, and with the broken people (dry bones) to whom Ezekiel ministered. They were confident that the biblical God was still acting in the affairs of nations to force the Pharaohs of that day to "let my people go." The Negro spirituals attest to their biblical interpretation of a protesting and liberating God.

Black people today throughout America can and should rediscover and recapture the liberating and destiny-shaping power of the biblical tradition, an affirmation unparalleled in all human history. Our foreparents plugged into it. Let us look at some of the images, stories, myths, and books in the Old Testament which when laid beside the Black American experience can serve liberation time in the Black community.

Points in the Old Testament Addressing Black Liberation

For the Black community in America, it is always two minutes before midnight, a few seconds before zero hour. It has no time to lose and a very little to use. It has a long way to travel and a short time to make it. Its liberation is long overdue. And the birth pressure calling the midwife is building all the time.

To deal with the Bible or anything else through Black eyes is to operate under the urgency of that pressure and from the content and genius of the Black experience. With this as a motive let us consider the following as points in the Old Testament which can inform and undergird Black liberation. We shall look at them in the context of responsible biblical interpretation.

The Myth of Cain and Abel

Now Adam knew Eve his wife, and she conceived and bore Cain, saying, "I have gotten a man with the help of the Lord." And again, she bore his brother Abel. Now Abel was a keeper of sheep, and Cain a tiller of the ground. In the course of time Cain brought to the Lord an offering of the fruit of the ground, and Abel brought of the firstlings of his flock and of their fat portions. And the Lord had regard for Abel and his offering, but for Cain and his offering he had no regard. So Cain was very angry, and his countenance fell. The Lord said to Cain, "Why are you angry, and why has your countenance fallen? If you do well, will you not be accepted? If you do not do well, sin is couching at the door; its desire is for you, but you must master it."

Cain said to Abel his brother, "Let us go out to the field." And when they were in the field, Cain rose up against his brother Abel, and killed him. Then the Lord said to Cain, "Where is Abel your brother?" He said, "I do not know; am I my brother's keeper?" And the Lord said, "What have you done? The voice of your brother's blood is crying to me from the ground. And now you are cursed from the ground, which has opened its mouth to receive your brother's blood from your hand. When you till the ground, it shall no longer yield to you its strength; you shall be a fugitive and a wanderer upon the earth" (Genesis 4:1-12).

This is a sacred myth * which can throw some light upon a question often raised by American Blacks as to the root of White brutality toward them. But to remain faithful to the rule of biblical interpretation laid down earlier, namely, to find out what it meant before saying what it means, let us give the result of research on the myth.

Scholars point out the following things about the original intent and meaning of this piece of sacred folklore. First, the myth was used by the narrator who put the strands together to show the long-range effect of human estrangement (breaking away) from God and God's redemptive plan. The root cause really began with the disobedience of Adam and Eve (humankind's prideful rebellion against God). Fratricide (the killing of a brother) always is the result of one's not being right with God. The breach or break between the person and God always results in a breach between person and person.

Second, the narrative had an additional intent of holding up the merits of the nomadic, pastoral life with its ethics of corporate life in contrast to the agricultural, settled life of the Canaanites with their fertility cults, nature gods, individualistic social order, and attempts to placate and control deity. In Israel God gave the orders regarding justice, group solidarity, * and mutual sharing. In Canaan, the people placated (paid off) and manipulated (twisted) Baal* (Canaanite god) into doing what they wanted.

Third, the myth reflected the belief held by several Semitic* peoples, that blood was the seat of life, and that human blood spilled had to be avenged. In other words, human life was sacred and of great worth. The whole divine design is upset by spilling human blood or taking human life.[5]

What does the legend mean to Blacks in America today in face of Black liberation time? First, it means that there is no great mystery as to why bigoted and racist White people or any other people engage in cruelty toward their fellow humans. When a person cuts himself/herself away from God, he/she floats on his/her ego, and when one floats on ego, one feeds on the pain and misery of fellow human beings.

There is no need either to engage in more time-consuming studies or to erect elaborate mythological theories to explain the roots of racism, bigotry, and brutality. There has been too much time spent on this kind of activity. Black people don't have the time to "study" White folk or to be studied by White folk. It is time for liberating action. Enough is already known as to why Cains always kill Abels. At gut level, the unreborn heart has a gravitational pull toward being "better than" the other person. This leaning toward better-thanness expresses itself in several forms: knowing more than, having more than, and appearing better than. Genesis 3:6 is very instructive: "So when the woman saw that the tree was good for food [having more than], and that it was a delight to the eyes [appearing better than], and that the tree was to be desired to make one wise [knowing more than], she took of its fruit and ate. . . ."

The second lesson for Black liberation in this legend is that Blacks must take clear note of the fact that Black people who cut themselves loose from God will brutalize their own Black brothers and sisters. Like the ancient Canaanites, Blacks who thrive on vested interest, greed, raw passion, and selfish individualism become harmful to the very kinds of social solidarity and mutual care so much needed in Black communities.

"Black Cains" can kill "Black Abels" by pushing, peddling, and consuming dope, thus physically and mentally destroying persons in

---

[5] Charles M. Laymon, ed., *The Interpreter's One-Volume Commentary of the Bible* (Nashville: Abingdon Press, 1971), p. 6; also, *The New Oxford Annotated Bible* (New York: Oxford University Press, 1973), footnotes, p. 6.

the Black community and drawing precious money from the Black community and giving it to some wealthy tycoon behind the scenes. Blacks can spiritually kill brothers and sisters by organizing prostitution for a profit instead of organizing restitution *as* a prophet. Blacks can destroy Blacks subtly by apathy, by vandalism, and by thumbing their noses at Black liberation efforts. Blacks need to avoid becoming like Cain.

The third insight to be drawn from the piece of sacred folklore is that Black folk must lift high the conviction that human life is sacred. We live in a world which has grown callous in its regard for human life. Women and children can be bombed and massacred; mass murders are committed; hostages are held and shot; and explosions are set off in buildings housing people. Assassinations have dotted the last two decades in this country, and lynching of minorities has not completely faded. It is no wonder that human life has come to be cheap in the minds of many.

The Black community cannot afford to allow itself to become infected by this attitude. Black people should be careful to examine new fads and new movements and not become mere reflectors of the latest trend. The good points in the Women's Liberation Movement notwithstanding, the contention that an abortion should be allowed solely on the decision of the pregnant woman not to carry the child cannot be supported. This view does not sound like the Black woman; it does not jibe with the historical position of the Black community about the value of human life.

Much in the "women's lib" kick is irrelevant to the Black woman in America anyway. Take, for instance, this business about a woman's being independent of and separated from the male. The problem of the Black woman in America has seldom been trying to "separate from" her man; her problem has been to stay glued to him and give him a sense of independence in spite of all the pressures he has had to live under day by day.

The Black community must have a great respect for human life in face of liberation time. There is even something healthy in the suspicion some Blacks have of planned parenthood, as legitimate as the concept appears, given the poverty condition in some Black areas. The money spent on twenty helicopters would feed all the Black babies born in this country last year.

Let the Black community draw wisdom from the legend of Cain and Abel.

The Book of Ruth

"Entreat me not to leave you or to return from following you; for where you go I will go, and where you lodge I will lodge; your people shall be my people, and your God my God; where you die, I will die, and there will I be buried. May the Lord do so to me and more also if even death parts me from you" (Ruth 1:16-17).

Bible readers for years have regarded the above passage as one of the sublimest statements in all the Bible, one which unveils a deep love and a profound family loyalty a daughter-in-law felt toward her mother-in-law. But the point of the author of this work went beyond showing genuine love between two members of a family. He had a bigger message, one which can underscore some wisdom for Black liberation in our time.

But first let the historical spadework be done. What was the intent of the author and how was the book understood by its first readers? As the Israelites moved along their historical journey, the interpretation of their destiny to be God's world-influencing instrument envisioned by the patriarch * Abraham and restated by Moses after the Sinai experience tended to fade from their agenda. They became narrow in their opinions of other people and their religions and customs. Some Israelite officials even placed a ban on Israelite marriages to non-Israelites. Association with people from other regions was frowned upon.

Therefore the Book of Ruth was written as a protest tract against such ethnic and religious narrowness. The book was a satire against the narrow reformers, showing that a Moabite woman could be found in the ancestry of David, the great Israelite king, and thus refuting the basis of the ban against ethnic intermarriage.[6] While the second aim of the author was to hold up for admiration the friendship and loyalty between two women, his main point was to contradict the dogmatic position against foreign blood.[7]

The work most likely consists of nonhistorical romantic details using small bits of historical material as the framework of the story. It tells of an Israelite family whose two sons married two Moabite women, foreigners, but both of the sons along with their father died

---

[6] The New Oxford Annotated Bible, p. 325. The Interpreter's One-Volume Commentary on the Bible, exegesis by Herbert G. May, pp. 150-152.

[7] Elmer W. K. Mould, Essentials of Bible History (New York: The Ronald Press Company, 1939), p. 415. See also Third Edition revised by H. Neil Richardson and Robert F. Berkey. Copyright © 1966 by The Ronald Press Company, New York.

leaving the three women as widows. One of the Moabite girls, after much agony, returned to her own people. But the other one who had grown so fond of and attached to her mother-in-law refused to part from her. Both women returned to Israelite territory where, due to the match-making skill of the Israelite mother-in-law, the daughter-in-law Ruth, eventually married a wealthy Israelite. According to Israelite folk history this union produced children who figured into the Davidic ancestry and the Messianic* line.

What does this work say to Blacks in liberation time? It throws light on the fact that efforts to segregate, restrict, ban, and proscribe the free movement and relationships of human beings is the doing of human beings and not of God. It makes no difference whether such is done in the name of God and pure religion, in the name of "pure blood," or in the name of some kind of self-defense; it is still an evil.

The rumblings of the Israelite reformers, Nehemiah and Ezra, however well-intentioned, sound curiously like the modern statements of members of the Ku Klux Klan or the White Citizens' Councils. Here is a passage from Ezra 9:2-3 (italics added):

> "For they have taken some of their daughters to be wives for themselves and for their sons; so that the *holy race has mixed* itself with the peoples of the lands. And in this faithlessness the hand of the officials and chief men has been foremost." When I heard this, I rent my garments and my mantle, and pulled hair from my head and beard, and sat appalled.

Well, the ranting of a bigot is the ranting of a bigot regardless of the auspices under which he does it.

Note how Nehemiah puts it as he, like Ezra, beats the table against interethnic relationships and marriages:

> In those days also I saw the Jews who had married wives of Ashdod, Ammon, and Moab; and half of their children spoke the language of Ashdod, and they could not speak the language of Judah, but the language of each people. And I contended with them and cursed them and beat some of them and pulled out their hair; and I made them take oath in the name of God, saying, "You shall not give your daughters to their sons, or take their daughters for your sons or for yourselves" (Nehemiah 13:23-25).

The members of the Black community then should draw two lessons from this work. The first is that they should never, never stand for groups, agencies, governments, institutions, organizations, or any other powers to throw in their way restrictions and bans based on race, blood, ethnic origin, religion, or economic status. Blacks have too long been victims of such action to limit their privilege and movement. For instance, governments have a legitimate right to block the spread of syphilis by requiring a blood test of two people who are to be married, but they have no divine right to dictate whom a person can marry.

The other lesson to be followed in the Black community is to cease copying the bigot's theories and methods. Stop trying to play God to your own people in the Black community. You see, liberation is an all or none thing. A brother cannot aid another brother in liberation by telling him that the magic formula has been brought to him and he has to obey like a sheep. Why should a brother be given only the choice of rejecting one kind of slavery for another? In other words, stop telling brothers and sisters with whom they can or cannot make friends, associate, work, love, and marry.

All theories and dogmas based on genes, races, "blood," ethnic makeup, color of skin, or any physical accident carry more evil than good and are ultimately proven wrong to say nothing of disastrous. For under God all genuine human ties cut across labels men and women make to pigeonhole people. All dogmas "against" God's human beings must "hang loose" in view of God's revelation tomorrow.

The Book of Daniel

> "My Lord delivered Daniel, Daniel;
> My Lord delivered Daniel,
> So why not deliver po' me?"
> (lines from a Negro spiritual)

In the Black community, when church congregations, quartets, and choirs sang the lines above, the song about Shadrach, Meshach, and Abednego and about King Belshazzar seeing the hand writing on the wall, the hearers somehow sensed that, with or without biblical scholarship, they had discerned what the Book of Daniel was all about. For the Black community was and is Daniel, or the three Hebrew boys, looking for that writer on the wall of history.

Still adhering to the rule of determining through background information the original meaning and setting, let us move ahead. One really has to return to the mind of Alexander the Great to understand Daniel. Alexander's tutor, Aristotle, had planted in the minds of his students the notion that Greek civilization and culture were supreme and that the rest of the world would remain backward and ignorant until it copied everything Greek. It appears that part of Alexander's motive for conquering the vast territory he did was to spread Greek culture. This he did with great zeal.

After his death, in spite of the fact that the empire carrying his name crumbled, some of his successors continued what scholars call the process of Hellenization (the Greeks called their country Hellas). But in some areas, particularly in Palestine, the job had to be done by force because the Jews, due to their proud history of religious loyalty and limited monarchy, balked at forced deculturalization. Riots and bloody uprisings occurred among the people. The government systematically set about its task and made resistance punishable by death. The Book of Daniel was written to urge the people to continue resistance and remain faithful to their ancient tenets, laws, and heritage. Bernhard W. Anderson writes:

> Shortly after the outbreak of the Maccabean wars, an unknown writer composed the book of Daniel. Undoubtedly he was one of the Hassidim, who felt a revulsion for the ways of Hellenism and the tyranny by which it was imposed upon the Jews. His purpose was to rekindle the faith of Israel, which was in danger of being extinguished by the aggressive and severe policies of the Seleucids, and to summon the Jewish people to unyielding loyalty even in the face of persecution. Affirming that the course of history was completely under Yahweh's sovereignty, he summoned his people to courageous faith. For when men believe that the issues are in the hands of God rather than in human hands, they can act without fear of the consequences. The book of Daniel, then, sets forth the theology of the Maccabean revolution. It has been rightly called "the Manifesto of the Hassidim."[8]

The Book of Daniel is a collection of six stories whose setting is in kingdoms and eras far removed from the author's own time (164 B.C.). The settings were backdated for security purposes. Each story followed the theme that the matter was in God's hands so that victory was assured, that the people were to remain faithful to their religion and culture and resist Hellenization.[9] They were given to understand that God would intervene to save as he had in the past, but even if death was the price of loyalty, martyrs would triumph in God's end-time. The pieces of religious fiction[10] involve the tales of Jewish youths who refused foreign diets, three young men who rebelled against conformity to foreign moral and political values and were

[8] Bernhard W. Anderson, *The Living World of the Old Testament* (London: Longmans, Green and Company, Ltd., 1957), p. 536.

[9] James Hastings, ed., *Dictionary of the Bible* (New York: Charles Scribner's Sons, 1963), pp. 199-200. Also see *The New Oxford Annotated Bible*, p. 1067.

[10] Elmer W. K. Mould, *op. cit.,* p. 434.

thrown in a fiery furnace, a hero by the name of Daniel who refused to alter his worship and was put in a lion's den, and a number of rulers who suffered the consequences of failing to acknowledge God's sovereignty. The book has a network of visions whose aim is to show God's sovereignty and final victory in and over history.

The lessons for the Black community flowing out of Daniel are simple but powerful. And there are four of them.

The first one is that Black oppression not only grates against the Black person's gullet, but it also runs against the grain of what God wants. For it is the very will of God that his human creatures be free, liberated, rescued, and whole in order to shape and enjoy this world which God has made. To be against Black liberation is to be against God. To work for freedom regardless of the risk is to walk and work in cadence with God. God's creatures, men and women, were not made to be slaves physically, mentally, emotionally, or otherwise.

The second lesson is that God backs up the cause and course of liberation and cannot lose. People can and should cooperate with God's liberation actions, but the ultimate course and victory are in his hands. God's victory is the wave of the future. Armed with this assurance, the Black community can risk and dare. It can walk forth on the promise of God. Liberation is sure, although those who would taste it must reach for it.

Third, the members of the Black community must sense and boldly affirm that God has already been with them in the midst of their suffering, like the fourth figure in the fiery furnace. He has aided their survival and confounded historians, sociologists, and anthropologists who marvel that the Black people neither remained helpless nor became extinct as had been predicted. Black people have been Daniels in the lions' den while God took the lions' appetites. They had to exist in states and communities ruled over by racist politicians, bigoted employers, brutal law enforcement units, night snipers, and churches which preached the Ham doctrine. But they are still here and are making themselves heard. The whole thrust of the Bible is that the God discerned therein is always here in the middle of things, working, fighting, redeeming, and liberating, if only those who would be free would lock hands with him and work shoulder to shoulder.

Lastly, out of Daniel comes the message that there is no one group on earth with norms to which everybody else has to conform. This includes regulations governing thought, methods, goals, food, dress, length of hair, ultimate allegiance, what one will revere. Gone is the day when one will be swayed by the saying "If it's White, it's right; if it's Black, get back." The Black person's being is just as legitimatized as that of any other.

The Book of Jonah

> "Ev'body talkin' 'bout heaven ain't goin' dere
>   Heaven, heaven.
> Ev'body talkin' 'bout heaven ain't goin' dere
> Gonna shout all over God's heaven."
> —a verse from a Negro spiritual

When Black field workers about 4:00 P.M. sang the song whose verse appears above, even the Black children sitting at the end of the rows of cotton or corn knew that the song had a code meaning. For Black folk have long known to take with a grain of salt, so to speak, the "evangelism" and religion of White folk whose actions contradicted their Black "soul saving" and their church talk. Undoubtedly this is why Albert Cleage wrote: "The white man's Church and religion are designed to meet *his* needs, not ours. We cannot borrow a Church which meets our needs from the white man." [11]

This brings us to the Book of Jonah. The book, like that of Ruth, is a protest tract against ethnic and religious bigotry. [12] It represented an attempt to chide or shame Israel back to the realization of her destiny as an instrument of God's universal saving grace. For in fact Israel was called to be God's instrument through which "all the nations of the earth would be blessed," even Israel's worst historical enemy, Assyria. In Genesis 12:3 God had said to Abram (later named Abraham): ". . . and in thee shall all families of the earth be blessed" (KJV). The author of Second Isaiah, speaking of Israel's destiny, in two places wrote:

> "I am the Lord, I have called you in righteousness,
>   I have taken you by the hand and kept you;
>   I have given you as a covenant to the people,
>   a light to the nations,
>   to open the eyes that are blind,
>   to bring out the prisoners from the dungeon,
>   from the prison those who sit in darkness" (42:6-7).

[11] Albert B. Cleage, Jr., *The Black Messiah* (New York: Sheed & Ward, Inc., 1968), p. 110.

[12] Mould, *op. cit.,* p. 416.

In 49:7 he wrote:

> Thus says the Lord,
>   the Redeemer of Israel and his Holy One,
> to one deeply despised, abhorred by the nations,
>   the servants of rulers;
> "Kings shall see and arise;
>   princes, and they shall prostrate themselves;
> because of the Lord. who is faithful,
>   the Holy One of Israel, who has chosen you."

But as the author of Ruth had sensed them, the writer of Jonah witnessed the bigoted effects of the Nehemiah-Ezra reforms.[13] The book was intended as a satire against the pride, self-righteousness, and ethnic aloofness of Israel in abandonment of her ancient destiny and purpose of being God's liberating and redemptive instrument for all people.

To convey his satirical message, the author formed a story around a character by the name of Jonah who was given orders by God to travel to Nineveh, the capital of Assyria, and deliver God's ultimatum that unless the city repented by a period of forty days, God would destroy it with fire and brimstone. Jonah at first refused to obey the order and took a ship heading in the opposite direction, perhaps with the hope that time would run out on Nineveh.

During the sea journey, a severe storm arose, and the ship's crew reasoned that the wrongdoing of someone on the ship had angered the god of the sea. By process of elimination, they concluded that the guilty one was Jonah. When Jonah confessed his disobedience, he was thrown overboard and swallowed by a huge fish. In his state of helplessness, Jonah begged for rescue and another chance and vowed in effect to obey God. God caused the fish to eject him onto the shore.

Then Jonah went to Nineveh and preached as he was ordered, but with the hope and expectation that the citizens would not repent and thus he would have the pleasure of seeing their destruction. So he went up on a hill and there sat down to watch. But the king of the city-state led the entire city in an act of repentance. This made Jonah very angry, and he sat sulking and pouting like a child with a temper tantrum. God pitied Jonah, swimming in his condescension, paternalism, and bigotry, and caused a gourd vine to grow to give him shade from the intense heat of the sun.

---

[13] Bernhard W. Anderson, *The Living World of the Old Testament,* pp. 424-425; Bernhard W. Anderson, *Understanding the Old Testament* (Englewood Cliffs, N.J.: Prentice Hall, Inc., 1966), pp. 524-525; Mould, *op. cit.,* p. 416.

But after a time, even God became "fed-up" with Jonah's attitude and had the vine cut down, chiding Jonah for his lack of human feeling when Jonah out of vested interest complained about God's destroying the vine. For Jonah could complain about the destruction of a vine but did not care about the destruction of human beings.

The main point of the author of this work was that Jonah was Israel who maintained a form of religious witness but who did not genuinely love the people to whom it witnessed. To Israel these other people were foreigners, outcasts, and heathens who deserved God's justice but were outside of the orbit of his mercy.

For the Black community gearing for liberation time, two instructive lessons come from Jonah. They can be summed up in the meaning of two elements in the Hebrew Passover, the unleavened bread and the bitter herbs, and from a statement attributed to Jesus of Nazareth that his followers should be as wise as serpents but as harmless as doves.

In the Passover ritual the unleavened bread (bread without yeast which is cooked more quickly) symbolized alertness. The people awaiting the signal to march did not have time to wait for the bread to rise. The bitter herbs symbolized the bitterness of oppression reminding those who had known it that they were to take care that they never slipped back into it; but also reminding them that they must always empathize and identify with others in misery (take care of the widows, the orphans, and the wayfarer) and never aid and abet such misery upon another.

Jesus' admonition was similar. Be alert (watch as well as pray), but always be empathetic and compassionate.

The first lesson then is that Blacks be alert to the fact demonstrated by the Black experience in America that not all persons who "missionize and evangelize" Blacks under the name of religion genuinely love Black people. A personal experience during college days illustrates the point. My first opportunity at college came as the result of the generosity and human concern of a small, Black-church-connected junior college in upstate South Carolina, which, like most such colleges in the South, presented about the only higher educational opportunity poor, Black students had then (1940s) and to a great degree have now.

The college's choir, under a very able director, received several invitations to sing during one year. Some of the invitations were from White congregations. One invitation was from a prominent White congregation at which the choir members expected the ogre of racial segregation to rear its head. The choir members, after promising the director that they would not walk out if segregation was encountered, accepted the invitation. As was expected, it happened. The hostess met the choir in the vestibule with the prearranged story that the church's sexton had cleaned the sanctuary that morning and in so doing had moved the piano from the sanctuary to a side room and had forgotten to move it back. So the choir was asked to sing from the side room out of view of the sanctuary.

Now, how many sextons move pianos from the sanctuary for a routine cleaning? And who could forget to replace an item as large and as vital as a piano in a church sanctuary? But the capstone of the story is that it was later learned that the program was developed by the church's missionary society to raise money to send to the Belgian Congo mission field. The idea was that they would collect money to give to Black missions but would not sit near Black Americans whose voices they would enjoy. This kind of White condescension and paternalism masked as religion has pervaded much of our land. Let Blacks be alert to this and not be afraid to point it out.

Another fact in the Black American experience to which Blacks should be alert is how many White Americans will often use diversionary slogans, codes, tactics, and causes to draw attention and action away from the weightier and more serious concerns on the socioethical and moral agenda. Like Jonah's hypocritical expression of concern for the gourd vine, many Americans have left the concern for social and economic justice, political equity, educational equality, and civil rights and have adopted concerns for "ecology," "law and order," "welfare reform," "reinstatement of the death penalty," "executive privilege," "strict constructionism," and "southern strategy."

Note that this country was the effective architect of the Marshall Plan to rebuild Europe, but it will not clear up the slums in its own cities. Black babies are going to bed hungry while America spends millions in military aid abroad. Large corporations gave millions toward the reelection of the president of the United States; how much did the same firms give to the United Negro College Fund? Millions can be appropriated for a Vietnam airlift but none for the systematic clearance of American slums.

The second lesson which the Black community can learn from Jonah is that, whether they presently realize it or not, Black folk in

America have a covenant with a mission from God which they must carry out. Their covenant with God, like Israel's, is based on the fact that God has brought them "a mighty long way." Their mission is to cooperate with God in their own liberation and thus help God liberate and save America. Black people have long reminded America that one cannot keep a person in a ditch without remaining there with him, so to speak; that when those on the lowest rung of the societal ladder are liberated and lifted, the whole people benefits.

The best in the Black American religious experience is the soul and the conscience of America, and the salt of the earth in America. The American Black churches as a whole never preached racial segregation, never substituted "soul saving" evangelistic fervor at the expense of the prophetic element in biblical tradition. In the days when few would hear, it cried in the wilderness for reconciliation under God even with White folk. And it did not wait for the legal rationale of the Supreme Court in 1954 and the Congress in the 1960s to declare that all human beings were equally God's children in the fullest sense of the affirmation.

The Book of Job

Ol' Job was the richest man
    that lived in the land of Nod;
He was the onliest man for miles aroun'
    that kept the commandments of God.

Chorus: There's nothin' you can do *(repeat)*
          To turn me 'round *(repeat)*
          I've done signed up *(repeat)*
          Made up my min' *(repeat)*
          I'm on my way, praise God,*(repeat)*
          I'm on my way.
                —an old Negro quartet song

Down through the history of this country those within the Black religious experience have tended to sense that the Book of Job was written as a message to people who had to live, survive, and hold on in spite of no pat answers to questions growing out of their misery and no sure solutions to their problems. But they knew one thing for sure—that they possessed determination and hope which came from some mysterious source which never dried up.

Some Black church people in the sixties and seventies have complained that the average White church member has neither the moral credentials nor the scholarly perspective to expound on Job to

Black people. They say that a White person by being a representative of a majority which shapes socioeconomic and political systems and structures in this country does not have the credentials to urge Blacks to follow the dictates of the book as it has been traditionally viewed and interpreted. They go on to point out that the traditional view often held by Whites is that the Book of Job was written to praise infinite patience under suffering without complaining or rebelling. These Blacks say that Black people have had more than their share of senseless, unmerited suffering as it is.

This complaint should not be dismissed lightly if at all. For the Book of Job was not written to tell people to "grin and bear it." An exception to much traditional White scholarship on Job is a little work done by L. D. Johnson, college minister at Furman University, in which the author points out that Job bristled and rebelled quite a bit in face of the pat answers and pet moral theories of his so-called friends.[14] We shall return to this later.

Biblical research reveals that the Book of Job is a poem mixed with prose narrative[15] which is classified with what reputable biblical scholars call the Wisdom Literature* (writings to guide one in practical living) group of writings. The intent of the author of the work was not an "attempt to explain the mystery of suffering or to 'justify the ways of God with men.' It aims at probing the depths of faith in spite of suffering."[16] B. W. Anderson maintains that the author provided the occasion for probing the question of *"the character of man's relationship to God."*[17]

Here are no philosophical or ready-made answers to suffering. Do not look for an examination of the nature of patience. The author is holding that the central issue in Israelite faith was the character of man's relationship to God.[18] Meaning in tragedy comes as the result of a genuine *meeting with God rather than speculation about God.* The Black American religious experience has long maintained this. Blacks had to cut through that which "made no sense." When the brother in the "amen corner" said, "You have to know God for yourself," this is what he was talking about—genuine encounter with God, something that went beyond "book knowledge" and "hearsay"

---

[14] L. D. Johnson, *Out of the Whirlwind, The Major Message of Job* (Nashville: Broadman Press, 1971).

[15] Bernhard W. Anderson, *Understanding the Old Testament,* pp. 508-510.

[16] *The New Oxford Annotated Bible,* p. 613.

[17] Anderson, *op. cit.,* p. 513.

[18] Mould, *op. cit.,* p. 411.

faith to the real experience of a personal meeting with God.

The Book of Job begins as if a curtain is raised on a drama showing God holding a council meeting. An uninvited spectator, Satan, barges into the meeting. God and Satan begin to josh each other. God brags to Satan about how loyal and upright his servant, Job, is. Satan comes back with the question: "Does Job fear God for nought?" (1:9), and quickly throws this challenge at God: "Have you not protected him on every hand, given him great success, property and wealth? Reach out now and take everything he owns and he will spit in your face" (Job 1:10-11, paraphrase).

God accepts the challenge and grants Satan permission to destroy Job's property, cattle, and even his children. When Job still holds up under the strain, Satan returns with a follow-up challenge to God: "Why not go for broke? Yes, every man has a breaking point and that is when something threatens his own life. Afflict his own person and he will do what I said he would" (see 2:4-5). God accepts the second challenge with the line drawn that Satan not take Job's life.

Satan then infects Job with a severe skin disease characterized by a combination of itch and pain. Job begins to complain bitterly that he does not deserve such suffering. His wife pokes fun at him. A group of his neighbors visit him assuring him that his suffering is the result of some great wrong he has committed and urging him to repent immediately.

Job reacts by challenging God to a debate, to a court hearing, in which God would prove to Job if he could, that he, Job, deserves such suffering. Later Job says that he is convinced that he does not deserve such treatment and asks why God, being the Sovereign he is, would choose him, a mere creature, as a whipping boy; what good does God get out of it? Why did God not destroy him at birth? He challenges God to stop hiding and show himself.

Finally God does grant Job a real meeting with him, not outside of his trouble but within it:

> "Then the Lord answered Job out of the whirlwind:
> 'Who is this that darkens counsel by words [speculation]
>   without knowledge [genuine encounter]?'"
>   (Job 38:1-2, bracketed words mine).

In face of the majesty of the genuine encounter with God, Job does not receive or further desire ready-made answers. He then sees life, not as a riddle to be answered but as a journey to be traveled; not as a chore to be terminated but as a venture to be dared; not as a prize awarded in security but as a challenge to contribute in the midst of creative insecurity.

The lesson for the Black community here is one which already at various points in the Black American experience has been affirmed. Without the genuine encounter with and sense of the *Mysterium Tremendum** or sense of the Holy, there can be no power for peoplehood, no daring liberation venture, no hope which contradicts present gloomy realities. Let the Black liberator ponder that every person has the breaking point of defeat, disillusionment, and despair without the genuine encounter with the Liberator God who empowers one to stand in the midst of trial and rebuff the storms of life.

This message of Job certainly is not a suggestion to Black people to cease attempting to find concrete and practical answers to problems which plague them from day to day. It does not mean that Blacks should try to escape through some form of religious withdrawal. What is strongly affirmed here is that, in the midst of the kingdom's work of Black liberation and peoplehood, Blacks, of all people, will have need of the spiritual (in the best sense of the term) and moral backbone to stand up to the "brick bats" which will come. No people can live trouble free even under fair circumstances. However, add being Black in America to the trouble all human beings face and multiply that by being a poor minority and see what our number says. We will have either the *genuine* strength of God on the one hand or drugs, alcohol, "rip-offs," and suicide on the other.

The Book of Exodus

> "Go down, Moses, way down in Egypt's land,
> Tell ol' Pharoah to let my people go."

This old spiritual whose origin goes further back than Blacks in this country can remember proves that Black Americans virtually adopted the book of Exodus as a kind of Black religious manifesto. Other songs, such as "Wade in the Water, Children," also attest to this. Call it the miracle of the Holy Spirit or call it by any other language, Black folk saw the Exodus escape as their own hope and identified themselves with the story. This understanding developed in spite of the huge effort to feed them diluted and twisted biblical interpretations. They believed that the same God who acted to free the Israelites from bondage was acting among them for liberation.

In light of biblical research and scholarship, it is noted that the author of Exodus aimed at showing how under divine guidance, direction, and power the Israelites, an enslaved people, were shaped into a unified people, led out of slavery by the strong hand of God who made a covenant with them to be his obedient nation under his full sovereignty and merciful guidance. But the author also was anxious to show that this liberation venture was no afterthought by God. This was part of God's long-range plan to redeem and call a people and through them redeem the world; this plan reached all the way back to Abraham, came down through Isaac and then Jacob whose tribes were given a land grant in Egypt by a government grateful for the economic security which an ex-Israelite slave brought to Egypt.

The author was eager for the Israelite reader to see God's hand shaping all the events and circumstances into his salvation or liberating plan.

The story begins by listing the Israelite clans which had been the recipient of the land grant in Goshen. After noting the population increase and some notable deaths of people of the old regime, the author penned a sentence on which the entire story thereafter hangs: "Now there arose up a new king over Egypt, who did not know Joseph" (Exodus 1:8).

Joseph was the ex-Israelite slave who improved Egypt's economy. The new government's perspective did not include the memory of that great deed. The new government saw the non-Egyptian as a military threat and a source of slave labor:

> And he said to his people, "Behold, the people of Israel are too many and too mighty for us. Come, let us deal shrewdly with them, lest they multiply, and, if war befall us, they join our enemies and fight against us and escape from the land." Therefore they set taskmasters over them to afflict them with heavy burdens; and they built for Pharaoh store-cities, Pithom and Raamses (Exodus 1:9-11).

But the Israelite population continued to increase in spite of the oppressive slave labor practices and genocide* which was instituted first through Israelite midwives, who dragged their feet, and later through Egyptian loyalists. The government ordered all Israelite males born to be drowned: "Then Pharaoh commanded all his people, 'Every son that is born to the Hebrews you shall cast into the Nile, but you shall let every daughter live'" (Exodus 1:22).

The story continues with an Israelite mother making a waterpoof basket in which she hid her male child near a royal bathing pool. The child was discovered and adopted by an Egyptian princess who unknowingly selected the child's real mother as his nurse. The child was named Moses and was educated in the royal palace. Being under the tutelage of his real mother, he no doubt knew his origin and heritage, for later his sympathies for his own enslaved people became evident. He killed a slave overseer.

After the slaying, he was declared a fugitive from justice by the Egyptian government and had to escape to an area called Midian where he lived with some tribes related to the Israelites. Moses married into one of the tribes and became a success at sheep raising. But the knowledge of the injustice and oppression under which his own people lived in Egypt haunted him and became a burning obsession with him, an issue branded on his mind which would not die.

He received a divine commission from the Liberator God, who hates human slavery and oppression, to return to Egypt and help shape Israel's liberation. This is how the author of the book painted the picture:

> And the angel of the Lord appeared to him in a flame of fire out of the midst of a bush; and he looked, and lo, the bush was burning, yet it was not consumed. And Moses said, "I will turn aside and see this great sight, why the bush is not burnt." When the Lord saw that he turned aside to see, God called to him out of the bush, "Moses, Moses!" And he said, "Here am I." Then he said, "Do not come near; put off your shoes from your feet, for the place on which you are standing is holy ground." And he said, "I am the God of your father, the God of Abraham, the God of Isaac, and the God of Jacob." And Moses hid his face, for he was afraid to look at God.
>   Then the Lord said, "I have seen the affliction of my people who are in Egypt, and have heard their cry because of their taskmasters; I know their sufferings, and I have come down to deliver them out of the hand of Egyptians, and to bring them up out of that land to a good and broad land, a land flowing with milk and honey, to the place of the Canaanites, the Hittites, the Amorites, the Perizzites, the Hivites, and the Jebusites. And now, behold, the cry of the people of Israel has come to me, and I have seen the oppression with which the Egyptians oppress them. Come, I will send you to Pharaoh that you may bring forth my people, the sons of Israel, out of Egypt" (Exodus 3:2-10).

Here Moses encountered the Liberator God, the God who had been actively involved in the affairs of people and nations through all generations. That he is always acting and making liberation happen is indicated by his identification of himself in this manner: "I AM WHO I AM" (3:14). In original Hebrew this can take the force of a verb of action as well as the verb to be. It can mean "I cause to happen" or "He causes to be." [19]

Moses, after having several of his excuses and negative alibis countered by God, went to Egypt and confronted the ruling dynasty which remained stubborn over a long period. Several calamities (plagues) resulted. Moses unified his people around a religious ritual symbolizing peoplehood (Passover), replaced their general mind-set of fear and defeatism with confidence and anticipation, shaped a plan of restitution, and waited for the final showdown with the government.

When a plague of death struck the country, strangely bypassing the Israelites, the Egyptian government gave in and agreed to the release of the slave-labor colony. But after the colony began its exit from the country, the government changed its mind and attempted to recapture it. In a manner so strange that historians are still trying to determine what happened, the Israelite colony was able to cross over a body of water which a few minutes later destroyed part of the Egyptian army in pursuit. The author of Exodus attributed it to the mighty hand of God. This experience became to the Israelites for all time proof positive that the Liberator God was directing this liberating event.

After the escape, the Israelites went into the wilderness and at Mount Sinai (or Horeb) accepted anew the covenant which God had made with their forefathers. The terms of the covenant (solemn agreement) were that God would continue, as he had revealed himself to be, as Sovereign Liberator, shaping and directing the destiny of a people he had called into a special instrumental relationship with him. The people pledged total loyalty and obedience to God, and ethical righteousness (justice, compassion, and humility) in human relations and the social order. [20]

The rest of the book deals with their rather nomadic (wandering) period in the wilderness, a period of woes and victories, of loyalty and defection. It was a period in which laws were shaped based on the codes received at Sinai (Ten Commandments) to fit the needs and aspirations of a people now faced with self-government and the uncertainties of a wandering existence. But, through it all, their destiny was kept before their eyes.

The book of Exodus says several things to the present Black

[19] *The New Oxford Annotated Bible,* footnotes, p. 70.
[20] Mould, *op., cit.,* p. 98.

situation in America. First, it reminds Black folk of the importance of heritage, total heritage. Today's Blacks dare not cut themselves off from their heritage by thumbing their noses at any part of the Black past. The Black religious experience is a most important part of that past. A contemporary Moses, the liberator of the present, must always understand that Abraham, Isaac, and Jacob knew and served the same Liberator God. And Moses cannot grow and succeed without the roots of his heritage.

It has become the "in thing" even for many Blacks in America to poke fun at the Black church because they do not truly know its past. The claim that all or most Black churches copied White churches just will not "hold water." The two churches have always, by the nature of our dual societies, had two different tasks.

As to theology, the White churches as a whole saw God as the caretaker of personal piety and comfort surrounded by a peaceful status quo, while the Black church had to see One who "plants his footsteps on the sea and rides upon the storms." "Storms" and raging seas form the constant experience of Black people.

The White church member, by and large, was in the "up" position looking down, whereas the Black member was "down" looking up. The White churches tended to restrict their concerns to "spiritual matters," for their political, economic, social, and educational structures supplied their needs. The Black churches had to concern themselves with all the needs of their people, social, economic, political, educational, and spiritual. A people ashamed of its past is confused about its present and afraid of its future.

A second lesson from Exodus for the Black community is that the Liberator God hates human slavery and oppression of all forms. It does not matter that the difference between the ancient Israelite quest and the present Black American quest is that Israel was seeking liberation "away from" the land of pain while the Black American is seeking liberation "within." Both seek release from human oppression. Human oppression always and in all times grates against God's will. God is just as displeased with it now as he was then. He is just as active against it now as he was then. He seeks men and women who will cooperate with him in causing liberation to happen.

Third, a people who would march with the Liberator God must be unified and united. They must genuinely hunger for liberation for themselves and for their fellows. They must genuinely empathize with and have an appreciation of the sacrifices, achievements, and sufferings of one another. They must be sensitive, alert, and passionately willing without counting cost. This is what the Passover ritual meant.

The last implication in Exodus for today's Blacks is that human justice and human freedom must precede law enforcement and social order. God's priorities are sometimes strange to those who want the grapes without cultivating the vines, so to speak. The author of Exodus does not bat an eye in affirming that God chose a fugitive from Egyptian justice to lead a liberation movement. That fugitive was Moses.

Law and order without the foundation of justice (allowing every person his or her due) and compassion (genuine concern for the needy and hurt) are always enforced by tyranny and oppression. The most lawful and orderly situations in the world are concentration camps.

God's Mouthpieces in Israel—The Prophets and Seers

Throughout the history of ancient Israel whenever the content of God's covenant with Israel was violated by persons regardless of their social, economic, or political status, there were rugged, bristling, "fire-eating," uncompromising figures who denounced their wrongs in the name of the covenant God. Like soldiers guarding a fort, these "watchmen" of God told it like it was while braving threat, violence, imprisonment, and death. Usually execution or lynching was required to stop them from standing up in public places or confronting some ruler and thundering, "Thus says the Lord God . . . !" These were the prophets and seers of Israel. Such were the prophetic heroes Samuel, Nathan, Elijah, Elisha, Amos, Isaiah, Micah, Hosea, and Ezekiel.

To understand fully what propelled these mouthpieces of God into their scalding rebukes, one needs to recall the nature and content of Israel's covenant faith. Remember that God agreed to continue doing what he had done and was doing—to be Sovereign Liberator and Shaper and Director of Israel's destiny which was to be God's world instrument through which all would come to know him. Israel, his people, pledged *total* recognition of and obedience to his Sovereign Lordship. Note: "I am the Lord your God, who brought you out of the land of Egypt, out of the house of bondage. You shall have no other Gods before me" (Exodus 20:2-3). Israel in addition agreed to maintain a particular social order characterized by justice, compassion, and humility. This what the biblical term "righteousness" means—just and right relations with one's neighbor.

Israel swore to this agreement. And whenever and wherever there was a violation of it, the prophet in Israel made himself heard. Sometimes the violation took the form of serving other gods or lifting other priorities above covenant priorities (idolatry); at other times the unfaithfulness involved mistreating or oppressing human beings.

Often in ancient Israel's experience, idolatry aided and abetted social injustice and vice versa. This problem was at the heart of the conflict between Canaanite society and religion and Israel's covenant faith. When Israel entered the Promised Land, she came face to face with the Canaanites, a settled, agricultural people who farmed and raised cattle. The Canaanites had a religious system (Baalism) centered around plant and animal fertility with a prescribed list of proper rites* to persuade their gods (these were a male and female, naturally) to act in the people's favor, increasing crops and herds. In their system there was little if any concern for an equitable or ethical human society.[21] The whole idea *was to keep the gods pleased and to make them produce* large herds and huge crop yields by engaging in the correct ritual. The Canaanite religious system had as its main aim to placate* and manipulate the gods to favor individuals in their vested interests.

On the other hand, the Israelite covenant faith was centered in the God (Yahweh) who refused to be placated and manipulated by ritualistic entertainment and pay-offs, but demanded full recognition of his sovereignty* to act according to his own will with full control of the destinies of people and nations. The covenant God also required ethical righteousness and social solidarity (the person in community.)

Herein lay the clash, the contrast, between the two systems. Elmer W. K. Mould, sizing up the Canaanite system, wrote that the greatest drawbacks in it were the separation of religion and morality and the smothering of the ethical concern (right action in human relations) with self-interest. Writes Mould:

> The divorce of religion from morality is the distressing side of the picture of this period, for religion concerned itself only with such matters as have been mentioned in the foregoing [personal gain and the appeasement of the gods]. If the feasts were properly observed, and sacrifices correctly and promptly offered, so that the deities were kept in good humor, man was satisfied. Man's prime concern in religion was with material benefits. . . .

[21]Bernhard W. Anderson, *The Living World of the Old Testament,* pp. 102-108.

How man treated his fellow man, and whether social and moral wrongs were righted or not, were matters deemed to be outside the sphere of religion.[22]

Mould went on to discuss the disrupting effect Canaanite religion had on some of the weak followers of the Israelite covenant faith:

Baalism went hand and hand with village patriotism. It exercised a disintegrating influence, separating village from village, and city from city. The Canaanites had no sense of social solidarity. Their ideal was individualistic. The well-being of all was sacrificed to the prosperity of the individual. The Hebrews took over many things from the Canaanites, and were in grave peril of absorbing this disunity also. In fact, much of the unity that Moses had succeeded in building up among the clans was lost in the early decades of life in Canaan. The unity Moses built up was founded upon the principle of loyalty to Yahweh. The author of Judges, in contending that the era he described was an era of apostasy, was exactly right. Baalism did make for disunity. The Hebrew social-ethical ideal always merged the individual in the group. The well-being of all was paramount in their thinking.[23]

Therefore the Canaanite system of religion (Baalism)* and its offshoots, coupled with the idol of the semi-divine nature of a suzerain or king, posed the greatest perverting threat to Israel's covenant faith. And the Israelite or Hebrew prophets declared war on the system and its influences in any form, for such a system did damage to the Sovereign of history and the social-ethical demands he made upon human beings.

Neither space nor balance will permit a thorough treatment of all the Israelite seers and prophets included in the Old Testament. The essence of prophetic religion will be summarized, noting that the prophets were the bold guardians of the covenant faith. Then some examples of their blistering and eyeball-to-eyeball confrontations with oppression, corruption, and immorality rooted in high places will be noted and applied to the present Black quest for liberation.

"Prophetic religion" is a term often used by some biblical scholars to mean the hard core of the Israelite covenant faith protected and put into words by the Hebrew prophets. This religious understanding is perhaps the purest strand of the covenant tradition. That is to say, the supporting priestly and ritualistic elements of the faith which developed through the centuries, while having functional value, were of secondary importance when compared with the core faith content

[22] Mould, *op. cit.*, p. 179.
[23] *Ibid.*, p. 180.

of recognizing God's lordship and sovereign judgment and abiding by his ethical and communal demands. So, stated in modern terms, the essence of prophetic religion lies in the following concepts.

First, the Sovereign God of history constantly calls into judgmental criticism all aspects of human living and world affairs. There is nothing or no one in heaven or on earth to be regarded as holy, sacrosanct, or untouchable save God himself. There are no persons, structures, systems, kingdoms, methods, or regulations which are above or even equal to God, and which cannot be called to accountability by God. He is King of Kings and Lord of Lords. All offices and positions, however highly elevated, must be subordinated to his throne. There is no divine right of kings, and all civil law must square with divine law to justify its right to exist. Might on earth does not make right in heaven.

Secondly, the right of every human being who honors God's sovereignty and ethical demands to live in brotherhood, free from oppression and brutality, is divinely granted and is not a privilege held in custody by people and governments to be doled out according to their pleasure. To live in wholeness and healing is a divine gift. Any violation is recorded in the divine log as theft against the Divine when such rights are snatched away from God's children.

Lastly, where there are human repentance, trust, and active obedience, there are God's mercy, redemption, and liberation. God will not liberate people without human cooperation. God is ever active in every present situation eliminating that which is against his will and bringing to pass what should be. His future is always open to healing and liberating. He opens the door to and grants the power for righteous and daring ventures. Tomorrow is always his. He is the Eternal.[24]

Briefly, here are a few examples of Israel's prophetic religion strands at work. First, let us note the conviction of God's critical sovereignty over rulers, structures, and affairs of man. King David, who reigned over Israel from 1016 to 976 B.C., was the nation's second monarch. He enjoyed great popularity, military success, and power. At one point, he used the power of his throne to take the wife of his military leader and compounded the wrong by ordering the general into a raging battle which resulted in his death.

---

[24] Cf. R. B. Y. Scott, *The Relevance of the Prophets* (New York: The Macmillan Company, 1944); J. Philip Hyatt, *Prophetic Religion* (New York: Abingdon-Cokesbury Press, 1947).

Nathan

At the point when David thought that his problem had been solved and his wrong sufficiently hidden, Nathan, the prophet, appeared for an audience with him. Nathan told David that he would tell him a parable about the questionable conduct of a rich man toward a poor man, and that he wanted the king's evaluation of the rich man's actions. David agreed to hear the story and evaluate the conduct.

The parable related that a rich man prepared a banquet for his guests, but instead of selecting an animal from his own numerous flock to feed his guests, he confiscated the only lamb of a poor family who had grown so attached to their animal that they kept it as a pet. At the end of the parable, Nathan asked David his opinion of the rich man. David, boiling with anger, declared that such a man deserved nothing short of death.

Here is a biblical account of what followed:

> Nathan said to David, "You are the man. Thus says the Lord, the God of Israel, 'I anointed you king over Israel, and I delivered you out of the hand of Saul; and I gave you your master's house, and your master's wives into your bosom, and gave you the house of Israel and of Judah; and if this were too little, I would add to you as much more. Why have you despised the word of the Lord, to do what is evil in his sight? You have smitten Uriah the Hittite with the sword, and have taken his wife to be your wife, and have slain him with the sword of the Ammonites. Now therefore the sword shall never depart from your house, because you have despised me, and have taken the wife of Uriah the Hittite to be your wife.' Thus says the Lord, 'Behold, I will raise up evil against you out of your own house; and I will take your wives before your eyes, and give them to your neighbor, and he shall lie with your wives in the sight of this sun. For you did it secretly; but I will do this thing before all Israel, and before the sun'" (2 Samuel 12:7-12).

David withered in confession, realizing that under Israel's God there is no king who can do as he pleases and no person, however powerful, who can escape divine judgment. There is no divine right of kings and rulers.

Elijah

Another example of Israel's covenant faith confronting high-hat rulers in the person of a prophet is the clash between Elijah and Ahab. Actually, here a prophet plants the seeds of a coup, a revolutionary overthrow.

King Ahab (875–853 B.C.) reigned over Israel as a member of the Omri dynasty which reinstated the policy which King Solomon had followed, that of forming political alliances by marrying princesses from surrounding kingdoms. Ahab was married to the daughter of Ethbaal, king of Sidon, and, from all indications, an absolute monarch. Ahab's queen, Jezebel, possessed a strong will, a high opinion of her beauty, and a philosophy that royal word and will became the law subject to no limitation. Jezebel was determined to be the power of the kingdom by not only establishing the power policies brought from her father's kingdom but also by making her own religion dominant in Israel. She worshiped Melkart, Baal of Sidon, and determined to destroy all religious competition in Israel by destroying the prophets of the covenant.

Nothing or no one was allowed to stand in her way. Her brutality and disregard for ethical consideration are related by the author of First Kings. A small landowner, Naboth, was contacted by King Ahab in an effort to persuade him to sell his plot of land to the throne. Naboth rejected the offer stating that the heritage regulations of his ancestors prevented his selling the land. The king was very displeased and related the matter to Jezebel, his wife. Jezebel, perhaps in an effort to show him how royalty got their way in her father's country, trumped up treason and blasphemy charges against Naboth which resulted in his being stoned to death. There was a law which allowed the throne to take over the property of persons executed for treason.

This crime brought the prophet Elijah upon the scene, thundering as he came. The story is that, after Naboth was stoned, his body was allowed to remain, and dogs consumed his corpse.

The author of First Kings relates what happened thereafter:

> Then the word of the Lord came to Elijah the Tishbite, saying, "Arise, go down to meet Ahab king of Israel, who is in Samaria; behold, he is in the vineyard of Naboth, where he has gone to take possession. And you shall say to him, 'Thus says the Lord, "Have you killed, and also taken possession?"' And you shall say to him, 'Thus says the Lord: "In the place where dogs licked up the blood of Naboth shall dogs lick your own blood"'" (1 Kings 21:17-19).

Later on, Elijah heaped similar condemnation upon Jezebel. He planted the seeds of a revolution which later under the prophetic fire of Elisha and the military leadership of Jehu toppled the house of Omri. To the Israelite prophet no ruler was above God. Of course, there were efforts then, as now, to persuade the prophets to become self-deluding yes-men who would shut their eyes for a price. Note Jeremiah, chapter 28. But the true prophet of God stood firm.

Isaiah

The Israelite prophets were just as solid in their attacks against oppression and exploitation of human beings. They stormed in the name of God against social and economic injustices which corrupt people in high places tried to cover up by the whitewash of religious motions.

In Isaiah 1:10-20, we read a scalding attack upon people who crush human beings and then run to worship service. Note the play upon the color of red in various shades intending to symbolize the blood of victims upon the hands of pretending worshipers held up in hypocritical prayer.

The passage reads:

Hear the word of the Lord,
  you rulers of Sodom!
Give ear to the teaching of our God,
  you people of Gomorrah!
"What to me is the multitude of your sacrifices?
  says the Lord;
I have had enough of burnt offerings of rams
  and the fat of fed beasts;
I do not delight in the blood of bulls,
  or of lambs, or of he-goats.

"When you come to appear before me,
  who requires of you
  this trampling of my courts?
Bring no more vain offerings;
  incense is an abomination to me.
New moon and sabbath and the calling of assemblies—
  I cannot endure iniquity and solemn assembly.
Your new moons and your appointed feasts
  my soul hates;
they have become a burden to me,
  I am weary of bearing them.
When you spread forth your hands,
  I will hide my eyes from you;
even though you make many prayers,
  I will not listen;
  your hands are full of blood.
Wash yourselves; make yourselves clean;
  remove the evil of your doings from before my eyes;
cease to do evil,
  learn to do good;
seek justice,
  correct oppression;

> defend the fatherless,
> > plead for the widow.
> "Come now, let us reason together, says the Lord:
> > though your sins are like scarlet,
> > they shall be as white as snow;
> though they are red like crimson,
> > they shall become like wool.
> If you are willing and obedient,
> > you shall eat the good of the land;
> But if you refuse and rebel,
> > you shall be devoured by the sword;
> > for the mouth of the Lord has spoken."

Amos

The prophet, Amos, of the eighth century B.C. is a classic example of how the prophets of Israel, in the name and covenant of Israel's God, became agitating instruments of divine judgment against social injustice and economic oppression. Neither national boundaries nor the snide criticism of fellow clergymen nor the power and "sacredness" of the political establishment stopped him from telling it like it was.

He declared that, because of the way the poor, the helpless, and the left-out were being ground into the dirt by the rich and powerful, God's verdict upon Israel would result in punishment swift and sure. No more would God hold off the sentence, he said. God's judgment upon those who walked on the needy and the crushed, who got rich off their misery, would be as sure as a builder's plumb line and as destructive as a parching drought or an insect invasion upon crops and grasslands. With his farmer's language and sheepherder's example, he took on even the royal palace in his righteous indignation.

Here are some of his utterances:

> Thus says the Lord:
> "For three transgressions of Israel,
> > and for four, I will not revoke the punishment;
> because they sell the righteous for silver,
> > and the needy for a pair of shoes—
> they that trample the head of the
> > poor into the dust of the earth,
> > and turn aside the way of the afflicted;
> a man and his father go in to the same maiden,
> > so that my holy name is profaned;
> they lay themselves down beside every altar

upon garments taken in pledge;
and in the house of their God they drink
    the wine of those who have been fined" (Amos 2:6-8).

Against the wealthy and extravagant women who in their greed
urged their husbands on in their corruption, Amos thundered:
"Hear this word, you cows of Bashan,
    who are in the mountain of Samaria,
who oppress the poor, who crush the needy,
    who say to their husbands, 'Bring, that we may drink!'
The Lord God has sworn by his holiness
    that, behold, the days are coming upon you,
when they shall take you away with hooks,
    even the last of you with fishhooks" (Amos 4:1-2).

Like Isaiah, Amos warned his neighbors of the futility of trying to
whitewash their social sins with religious services. He represented
God as saying:

"I hate, I despise your feasts,
    and I take no delight in your solemn assemblies.
Even though you offer me your burnt offerings
    and cereal offerings,
    I will not accept them,
and the peace offerings of your fatted beasts
    I will not look upon.
Take away from me the noise of your songs;
    to the melody of your harps I will not listen.
But let justice roll down like waters,
    and righteousness like an everflowing stream" (Amos 5:21-24).

Micah

Another prophet, Micah, became fed up with corruption in "high
places," in the leadership ranks of both religion and politics in both
Israel (whose capital was Samaria) and Judah (whose capital was
Jerusalem). Bribery, intrigue, and conspiracy, usually at the expense
and injury of the "little people," were the order of the day.

This is how Micah saw it all:

Hear, you peoples, all of you;
    hearken, O earth, and all that is in it;
and let the Lord God be a witness against you,
    the Lord from his holy temple.
For behold, the Lord is coming forth out of his place,
    and will come down and tread
    upon the high places of the earth.

And the mountains will melt under him
and the valleys will be cleft,
like wax before the fire,
like waters poured down a steep place.
All this is for the trangression of Jacob
and for the sins of the house of Israel.
What is the trangression of Jacob?
Is it not Samaria?
And what is the sin of the house of Judah?
Is it not Jerusalem? (Micah 1:2-5).

To corrupt rulers with power in their hands Micah stated:

Woe to those who devise wickedness
and work evil upon their beds!
When the morning dawns, they perform it,
because it is in the power of their hand.
They covet fields, and seize them;
and houses, and take them away;
they oppress a man and his house,
a man and his inheritance.
Therefore thus says the Lord:
Behold, against this family I am devising evil,
from which you cannot remove your necks;
and you shall not walk haughtily,
for it will be an evil time (Micah 2:1-3).

These blistering words were delivered against the officeholders and "fathers of the nations" who made a mockery of the trust and proper functions which should have characterized their positions by taking bribes and crushing the helpless:

Hear, you heads of Jacob
and rulers of the house of Israel!
Is it not for you to know justice?—
you who hate the good and love the evil,
who tear the skin from off my people,
and their flesh from off their bones;
who eat the flesh of my people,
and flay their skin from off them,
and break their bones in pieces,
and chop them up like meat in a kettle,
like flesh in a caldron.
Then they will cry to the Lord,
but he will not answer them;
he will hide his face from them at that time,
because they have made their deeds evil.
Thus says the Lord concerning the prophets
who lead my people astray,

who cry, "Peace"
    when they have something to eat,
but declare war against him
    who puts nothing into their mouths.
Therefore it shall be night to you, without vision,
    and darkness to you, without divination (Micah 3:1-6).

And, true to the full prophetic line, Micah also reminded the people who had violated the covenant faith that they would not be able to hoodwink God by paying him off with religious ritual. This passage has become a prophetic classic:

"With what shall I come before the Lord,
    and bow myself before God on high?
Shall I come before him with burnt offerings,
    with calves a year old?
Will the Lord be pleased with thousands of rams,
    with ten thousands of rivers of oil?
Shall I give my first-born for my transgression,
    the fruit of my body for the sin of my soul?"
He has showed you, O man, what is good;
    and what does the Lord require of you
but to do justice, and to love kindness,
    and to walk humbly with your God?" (Micah 6:6-8).

As was stated earlier, the prophetic stand against high-minded rulers, tyrannical systems, and oppressive powers is nothing short of dynamite. When one realizes that Black people may be driven away from the liberating power of the Bible because of the mishandling and twisting of its message and content by the corrupt and ignorant, the chances are that one is apt to sink into deep despair.

Ezekiel

Not only does prophetic religion affirm in the strongest terms God's sovereign judgment upon everything and the divine right of the human being to live a life of wholeness, but it also carries the conviction that God constantly beckons people into his healing future of redemption and liberation regardless of the present circumstances and conditions. The prophet Ezekiel (593-573 B.C.) had the terrible task of getting members of a concentration camp to adopt such a conviction.

Ezekiel himself stated that the task almost overwhelmed him: "The Spirit lifted me up and took me away, and I went in bitterness in the heat of my spirit, the hand of the Lord being strong upon me; and I came to the exiles at Telabib, who dwelt by the river Chebar. And I sat there overwhelmed among them seven days" (Ezekiel 3:14-15).

But later on, when Ezekiel "got himself together" by the power and perspective of the covenant faith, he rallied the Israelite exiles. Here was a group of conquered and uprooted people, eaten by a combination of guilt, despair, and bitterness.[25] But the famous parable of the dry bones (chapter 37) pictures the new life which many received as a result of their rediscovery of the covenant faith. When human repentance and active obedience meet God's ever-present, liberating power and grace, the new future is opened.

This is part of Ezekiel's symbolic account:

> Then he [God] said to me, "Son of man, these bones are the whole house of Israel. Behold, they say, 'Our bones are dried up, and our hope is lost; we are clean cut off.' Therefore prophesy, and say to them, Thus says the Lord God: Behold, I will open your graves, and raise you from your graves, O my people; and I will bring you home into the land of Israel. And you shall know that I am the Lord, when I open your graves, and raise you from your graves, O my people. And I will put my Spirit within you, and you shall live, and I will place you in your own land; then you shall know that I, the Lord, have spoken, and I have done it, says the Lord" (Ezekiel 37:11-14).

Under the hand of the biblical God, nothing stays as it is; in the tug of his power, conditions are not static and possibilities are not limited. But even beyond the present, God's future is qualitatively greater. The God of the covenant faith takes the active obedience of those who would be liberated and makes tomorrow better than today.

Jeremiah

Up to this point, emphasis has been placed on the two-sided nature of the covenant faith of Israel, the agreement between God and Israel in which God promised to continue to do what he had done—to call, liberate, and direct Israel and redeem (liberate) other nations through her. Israel's side of the agreement was to recognize at all times *total, active allegiance* to God as her Sovereign and judging Lord and to give total obedience to his *ethical demands.* The biblical record is that God kept his side of the agreement, but Israel caused a rupture of the agreement by failing to honor her side.

The reason for this emphasis, aside from the fact that it is the biblical emphasis, is that the covenant faith speaks with power to the

---

[25] Note Psalm 137 to sense the depth of their despair and hatred of their conquerors.

Black liberation effort. Not only does the covenant faith embraced by Israel affirm that God *will act to liberate;* but it also affirms that a half-covenant is no covenant at all. That is to say that if the people in the agreement cease to be passionately active, alert, just, and compassionate, the power of the covenant is blocked and liberation is postponed. The process is similar to the interaction found in giving a gift. Before the act of giving can be completed, not only must there be a giver, but there also must be a receiver. If the would-be receiver never takes the gift, the giver can never complete the act of giving. There must be a *reaching for* what is given.

Therefore, in the same way a people must exert the obedient effort of *reaching for* what God promises and *reaching for* what the needy brothers and sisters need. It will be found that the two are harmonious, are two sides of the same coin. He who prays for the crop must plow the field and share the grain.

Yet the problem of why human beings break the divine covenants has been probed by sages throughout the history of man. Why are so many people blind, lazy, cowardly, and cruel even after having promised that they will henceforth be alert, obedient, brave, and compassionate?

The prophet Jeremiah offered an answer to the question and a solution to the problem. In his agony over Israel's broken promise in the covenant, he finally said that the majority of the Israelites, or the nation as a whole, never really received the covenant faith at gut level, at the heart of what "made them tick." Jeremiah said, in effect, that they never internalized the covenant faith. There was never that necessary, total self-giving to the faith cause; there was never the thing which "grabbed" the whole person, the revolutionary shaking up of the person, the "new birth."

Though Jeremiah was often in states of despair which caused him to weep, he saw God offering a remedy for the problem.

Here are Jeremiah's words:

"Behold, the days are coming, says the Lord, when I will make a new covenant with the house of Israel and the house of Judah, not like the covenant which I made with their fathers when I took them by the hand to bring them out of the land of Egypt, my covenant which they broke, though I was their husband, says the Lord. But this is the covenant which I will make with the house of Israel after those days, says the Lord: I will put my law within them, and I will write it upon their hearts; and I will be their God, and they shall be my people. And no longer shall each man teach his neighbor and each his brother, saying, 'Know the Lord,' for they shall all know me, from the least of them to the greatest, says the Lord; for I will forgive their iniquity, and I will remember their sin no more" (Jeremiah 31:31-34).

The affirmation is that the covenant God who liberates, calls, and directs the destinies of those who cleave to him can actually rehabilitate, empower, and reshape human hearts (attitudes, wills, desires, allegiances, self-concepts). Is this not needed in the Black communities? Will Blacks in America remember or rediscover the covenant made with the biblical God by Black ancestors—a covenant ignored by many Blacks since God took Black foreparents by the hand and led them out of slavery, through Reconstruction, through the Depression, and through the turbulent fifties and sixties?

Blacks in America then should take a look at that "new covenant" and what it produced and what it is still doing. This brings us to the New Testament (which in the original Greek can be translated "new covenant"—see Luke 22:20). As has been stated continually, the God revealed in the Bible never ceases to act to liberate, call, empower, and direct—even when he is rejected. He is ever-present, ready to enter a viable covenant. When old covenants are violated, God initiates new ones. Under God there are always new avenues. The faithlessness of Israel did not stop the incarnation. The rupture of the covenant initiated by God with Abraham and later renewed at Sinai did not stifle God's liberating and redeeming activity, for Jesus of Nazareth, the central figure of the New Testament, saw himself as ushering in God's "new covenant" for liberation, redemption, and wholeness.

Questions for Further Study

1. What comparisons and contrasts can be found when one places the Black American religious experience alongside that of ancient Israel's?
2. What in your opinion caused the Black American to discern the liberating implications of the Bible in spite of efforts in America to use the Bible to justify slavery and racial segregation?
3. How can the protest books of Ruth, Jonah, and Daniel inform the Black struggle today?
4. Why in your opinion did the story of the Exodus and the exploits of the Israelite prophets make an impact upon the aspirations of the American Black community?

5. Does the book of Job really counsel patience in all situations? Can you find other meanings in Job?
6. In what ways can the thesis that the covenant idea exists throughout the Bible be defended?

Additional Reading

Anderson, Bernhard W., *The Living World of the Old Testament* (London: Longmans, Green and Co., Ltd., 1957).

Johnson, L. D., *Out of the Whirlwind: The Major Message of Job* (Nashville: Broadman Press, 1971).

Rauschenbusch, Walter, *Christianity and the Social Crisis* (New York: The Macmillan Company, 1907).

Scott, R. B. Y., *The Relevance of the Prophets* (New York: The Macmillan Company, 1944).

The New Testament and the Black American

3

The New Testament consists of a group of writings produced in first- and second-century Palestine and Asia Minor (Philippians and Philemon were written from Rome) by persons on whom Jesus of Nazareth and the events surrounding him had a great liberating and transforming impact. Jesus' birth, teachings, and actions created a powerful freedom-and-action movement mostly among the poor, the "common people," and the outcasts.

But two events in particular had a tremendous influence upon Jesus' followers, aside from his teachings and actions. Jesus was executed. And, for a short period thereafter, his followers scattered and went into hiding. Then there spread among the group a powerful conviction that drove away their fear and unified them. The group went about telling everyone who would listen that God had raised Jesus from death, that in some mysterious but real sense Jesus was now alive among them.

To Jesus' followers, this resurrection * from the dead became proof that God was backing everything that Jesus taught, did, and stood for. In fact, they reasoned that God had sent Jesus into the world as part of his liberation plan. Second, for them the resurrection proved that God's liberation plan which is built into his whole program was not only continuing but also was in Jesus, the Christ, "picking up steam" in the last lap for the finish line, so to speak. Third, the resurrection to these followers meant that *absolutely nothing* could defeat God, his liberation programs, and his followers, in the long run. For God had even overturned death which is the worst defeat. Death, which had "looked like" the total and complete destruction of all meaning, all hope, and all dreams, had now been exposed as a weak bully, they said.

Many members of the group increasingly became braver and more active. They made fiery speeches, defied oppressive governments, boldly risked death, and refused to denounce publicly their convictions. Other members fled to caves and underground cemeteries (catacombs) but did not cease their activities.

These then were the people for whom most of the New Testament writings were intended. Some authors among them were attempting to put in logical and orderly form what God was doing in and through Jesus for human beings who were slaves to evil in both its internal forces (guilt, fear, despair, self-hatred, bigotry, animosity, and greed) and external power (oppressive and unjust governments, inhumane regulations, dehumanizing religious and social structures, poverty, diseases, and corrupt leaders). Other authors wrote to deal more specifically with problems which arose. But they all wrote to edify and inspire those of the "bond of Christ."

One main conviction which all the New Testament authors shared was that Jesus was the master link in God's liberation and redemption plan. To them Jesus was the point of direct divine contact and the apex of what God is doing in human history, bringing the world in line with his will. The apostle Paul wrote to the Galatians regarding the matter: "But when the right time finally came, God sent his own Son" (Galatians 1:4, TEV). The author of Ephesians wrote: "God did what he has purposed, and made known to us the secret plan he had already decided to complete by means of Christ. God's plan, which he will complete when the time is right, is to bring all creation together, everything in heaven and on earth, with Christ as head" (Ephesians 1:9-10, TEV).

When reading the New Testament (as also with the Old Testament), one must remember that the authors and their readers lived in a prescientific era. Very few people then knew of or discussed what we call "physical laws." In their efforts to explain their experiences, convictions, hopes, and fears, they used the thought patterns, terms, and categories of explanation of their own time. They were influenced by the mind-sets of their own era. They had no trouble with blending what we call today "biology" and "theology"; so they could say that the divinity of Jesus Christ was preserved by God by his having the Holy Spirit make Jesus' mother pregnant rather than having a man do it the ordinary way. Thus, they explained their belief that Jesus was both divine and human.

It was common in those days for people to believe that heavenly creatures visited earth, that demons caused illness and insanity, and that God suspended ordinary operations in the world to do special things from time to time. But the realities and experiences which these people attempted to explain were present then and are present in our lives today.

Likewise the people of that time knew nothing about what we call writing "objective" biography or history. They blended feelings and convictions with events and facts as a matter of course. Therefore the Gospels, for instance, are faith portraits of Jesus, woven from documents and eye-witness reports circulated earlier. Their authors' angle of vision carried the conviction that Jesus was God's commissioned agent (Messiah–Christ–Anointed One–Son of man) directly sent with God's full nature, power, and authority (own Son) through whom God is bringing all things back in line with his will. Paul wrote to the group at Corinth: "All this is from God, who through Christ reconciled us to himself and gave us the ministry of reconciliation; that is, in Christ God was reconciling the world to himself" (2 Corinthians 5:18-19a).

The New Testament then is a collection of writings which affirm that the God who created the world and made a covenant with Abraham, Moses, and Israel has broken into the human scene in a most powerful and special way through Jesus to liberate again (new covenant), call (church), direct, and empower (Holy Spirit) a people for himself. The affirmation from Matthew to Revelation is that God's liberating and redeeming work will win out, to the full glory of God. The author of the Fourth Gospel summed up God's special incoming through Jesus, referring to Jesus' mediation role by use of the Greek philosophical term "Word": "The Word became a human being and lived among us. We saw his glory, full of grace and truth. This was the glory which he received as the Father's only Son" (John 1:14, TEV).

Jesus, the Central Figure

Now in the time of Black liberation, Black brothers and sisters should use the results of the best research to get to know the liberating thrust of the New Testament. And since Jesus is the central figure of the New Testament, they should concentrate on him.

The following questions regarding Jesus should be raised and answered. Since the golden thread throughout the biblical saga is the covenant between God and his people, what was Jesus' relationship to and understanding of the covenant? What did Jesus see as his mission? What were Jesus' priorities particularly with reference to human beings? What were his religious, moral, and ethical imperatives?

Jesus and the Covenant

Jesus of Nazareth was a product of Hebrew heritage and therefore a son of the Israelite covenant. He was steeped in the knowledge of Israel's prophetic tradition and was often known to quote from prophetic and other writings of the Old Testament. He shared and even expanded the conviction that the God of his ancestors works in history from a live purpose toward an ultimate goal, and that God's purpose and goal involved creation, revelation, and liberation.

Jesus shared further with his fellow Hebrews that God's historical covenant with them involved the reciprocal pledges between God and the people—God pledging liberation and guidance, and the people pledging total and active obedience and ethical righteousness (justice, compassion, and humility in human relations). He believed that a people must seriously take God at his word (faith) by alertly striving to cooperate with God's liberating action and will. This willingness to move with God packs tremendous power, according to him. Faith as small as a mustard seed could figuratively move mountains.

But Jesus applied to the covenant faith a wisdom which grew out of the agony over the question of why people broke covenants with the living and liberating God, making it necessary for God to renew covenants and reempower people for liberation from age to age. Taking a position similar to Jeremiah's, Jesus maintained that a person's loyalty and dedication to God's liberating plan must flow freely and spontaneously. Otherwise, he held, these qualities are not genuine. Jesus went on to affirm, as had Jeremiah, that only the redemptive and liberating power of God could and would break the dam and liberate the springs of human loyalty to God's plan.

In other words, the power of God, according to Jesus, liberates one at the core of one's being, in that area where attitudes, motives, drives, emotions, and passions make contact with what is both real and good. One may call it "rebirth," "conversion," "inner freedom," "soul force," or whatever. There must be genuine inner liberation as well as external liberation. Mental and emotional chains, such as fear of death, self-hatred, egomania, ingrained distrust of brothers and sisters, slave mentality, greed, and apathy must be uprooted from the soul before one can work shoulder to shoulder with the liberating God.

Jesus also understood himself as rescuing the divine liberation plan from all of the covenant failures up to his day. He felt that God was renewing through him and his followers a "new covenant" so solemn that it was sealed with his blood. Luke records that during Jesus' last Passover* celebration with his followers he said: "This cup is God's new covenant sealed with my blood which is poured out for you" (Luke 22:20, TEV). Jesus saw himself and his program as an intensified continuation of God's mighty liberation activity in human history.

It is interesting to note that Jesus was convinced that God's covenant plan for liberation could never be defeated by the violence and brutalities of oppressions. Such violent attacks would in a strange sort of way aid the divine plan. The author of the Gospel of John reports Jesus as saying: "I tell you the truth: a grain of wheat remains no more than a single grain unless it is dropped into the ground and dies. If it does die, then it produces many grains. Whoever loves his own life will lose it; whoever hates his own life in this world will keep it for life eternal" (John 12:24-25, TEV). This is not a suggestion of self-hatred; it is a reminder that in God's great cause of liberation the blood and self-sacrifice of martyrs have always been the fertilizer of the kingdom's progress. To the degree that Blacks learn and follow this principle, Black liberation will become a reality.

Jesus' Main Driving Force

What was Jesus' main driving force? What made him tick? Where was he coming from? Everything Jesus said, did, stood for, and stood against was directed from a gut-level conviction, rooted in his religious tradition and experience and his unique human compassion, that the human being was uniquely important to God and was due justice, compassion, full life, and liberation as a top, divine priority. This is why the Gospels picture him as being intensely interested in the plight of the poor, the dispossessed, the exploited, the mistreated, and those who were held in low esteem.

Modern theologians and preachers have coined the phrase that Jesus was "a man for others." A German theologian, Dietrich Bonhoeffer, in a Nazi concentration camp scribbled some notes for a book which he was never able to write before he was put to death. This is one of his notations: "Encounter with Jesus Christ, implying a complete orientation of human being in the experience of Jesus as one whose only concern is for others. This concern of Jesus for others [is] the experience of transcendence."[1]

The passion for going all-out for a fellow human being was a main characteristic of Jesus' makeup. His indignation often flared when he witnessed the mistreatment of people. To the straight-laced modern, one of the most embarrassing passages of the New Testament is the incident of Jesus' cleansing of the temple. The Gospel writer Mark wrote:

> When they arrived in Jerusalem, Jesus went to the temple and began to drive out all those who bought and sold in the temple. He overturned the tables of the moneychangers and the stools of those who sold pigeons, and would not let anyone carry anything through the temple courts. He then taught the people, "It is written in the Scriptures that God said, 'My house will be called a house of prayer for all peoples.' But you have turned it into a hideout for thieves!" (Mark 11:15-17, TEV).

A similar report is found in Matthew 21:12-13.

One needs little imagination to sense that there was a "hot time" there that day. Any incident that would cause merchants and bankers to flee and leave their money and wares would have to be persuasive, to put it mildly. Dr. Harry Emerson Fosdick has pointed out that Jesus was indignant, not just because there was buying and selling, but because the business being transacted was dishonest. The money-changers exchanged foreign money for the temple shekels at a profit. Sacrificial animals were sold at exorbitant prices because only animals sold in the temple were sure to be found without defect. While four cents apiece was the normal price for pigeons, the temple traders charged as much as $1.95 for a pigeon. So Jesus drove out

---

[1] Dietrich Bonhoeffer, *Letters and Papers from Prison,* ed. Eberhard Bethge (New York: The Macmillan Company, 1962), p. 237.

those who carried on this kind of business in the court of the temple.[2]

In that same spirit of "going to bat" for people who were stepped on, Jesus elevated women whose status in his day was slightly above that of slaves. Mark records:

> Some Pharisees came to him and tried to trap him. "Tell us," they asked, "does our Law allow a man to divorce his wife?"
>
> Jesus answered with a question, "What commandment did Moses give you?"
>
> Their answer was, "Moses gave permission for a man to write a divorce notice and send his wife away."
>
> Jesus said to them, "Moses wrote this commandment for you because you are so hard to teach. But in the beginning, at the time of creation, it was said, 'God made them male and female. And for this reason a man will leave his father and mother and unite with his wife, and the two will become one.' So they are no longer two, but one. Man must not separate, then, what God has joined together" (Mark 10:2-9, TEV).

From our modern vantage point, it may be difficult to see what a radical elevation of women this viewpoint represented. Keep in mind, however, that then wives were slightly more than possessions. In practical terms this meant that a man could declare his wife unacceptable for any small reason or whim with little challenge. She could be cast out with little chance for security and economic survival.

On the status of women in early Hebrew thought, Elmer W. K. Mould wrote:

> Evidence of progress in social standards is seen further in the laws which reveal the status of women. The early Covenant code deals first with the status of slaves (Ex. 21:2-6), and *next* with that of women (21:7-11)! A woman was a piece of property. If a man bought a wife, he could not resell her to another man, but if a man bought a slave girl, he could resell her to another Hebrew when he chose. That was the whole difference between the wife and the female slave.[3]

Lindsey P. Pherigo, commenting on the passage in Mark in the *Interpreter's One-Volume Commentary on the Bible,* points out that "Rabbi Hillel taught and practiced a very lenient interpretation of Deut. 24:1, permitting men to divorce their wives for minor matters."[4] Also, a woman in Jesus' environment could not divorce

[2] Harry Emerson Fosdick, *Jesus of Nazareth* (New York: Random House, Inc., 1959), pp. 143-144.

[3] Elmer W. K. Mould, *The Essentials of Bible History* (New York: The Ronald Press Company, 1939), p. 285.

[4] Charles M. Laymon, *The Interpreter's One-Volume Commentary on the Bible* (Nashville: Abingdon Press, 1971), pp. 661-662; *The New Oxford Annotated Bible,* p. 1227.

her husband. It then seems reasonable to conclude that, since it was the man's and not the woman's prerogative to sue for divorce and since the woman's status was the precarious or shaky one, the whole thrust of Jesus' position was to elevate the woman both by declaring her a divinely intended *partner,* originally intended in creation, and by holding that a man should not cast her out except for reasons as serious as adultery.

In his passion for a fair shake for the human being, Jesus often drew ridicule and threats by his conviction that other ethnic, racial, and national groups enjoyed equal status before God. One sabbath, after worship service, a congregation turned into a lynch mob which attempted to kill him because he stated that God cared for Sidonites and Syrians as well as Hebrews.

The author of the Gospel according to Luke wrote:

> "I tell you this," Jesus added. "A prophet is never welcomed in his own home town. Listen to me: it is true that there were many widows in Israel during the time of Elijah, when there was no rain for three and a half years and there was a great famine throughout the whole land. Yet Elijah was not sent to a single one of them, but only to a widow of Zarephath, in the territory of Sidon. And there were many lepers in Israel during the time of the prophet Elisha; yet not one of them was made clean, but only Naaman the Syrian."
>
> All the people in the synagogue were filled with anger when they heard this. They rose up, dragged Jesus out of town, and took him to the top of the hill on which their town was built, to throw him over the cliff. But he walked through the middle of the crowd and went his way (Luke 4:24-30, TEV).

Many of Jesus' townspeople scorned his associations with the "half-breeds" of their society. Jesus responded by holding these people up as examples of genuine piety. This group, known as Samaritans, stemmed from the centuries of intermarriage between Hebrews and non-Hebrews. Such intermingling was prohibited by Hebrew law and custom which were intensified, it will be recalled, by the reforms of Ezra and Nehemiah.

Jesus often responded with stories in which the hated one was the hero or the compassionate one. In a response to a loud-mouth legal expert, Jesus told this story illustrating what genuine human compassion really is:

> "There was a man who was going down from Jerusalem to Jericho, when robbers attacked him, stripped him, and beat him up, leaving him half dead. It so happened that a priest was going down that road; when he saw the man he walked on by, on the other side. In the same way a Levite also

came there, went over and looked at the man, and then walked on by, on the other side. But a certain Samaritan* who was traveling that way came upon him, and when he saw the man his heart was filled with pity. He went over to him, poured oil and wine on his wounds and bandaged them; then he put the man on his own animal and took him to an inn, where he took care of him. The next day he took out two silver coins and gave them to the innkeeper. 'Take care of him,' he told the innkeeper, 'and when I come back this way I will pay you back whatever you spend on him'" (Luke 10:30-35, TEV).

Luke also records another incident which show Jesus' attitude on the matter:

As Jesus made his way to Jerusalem he went between Samaria and Galilee. He was going into a village when he was met by ten lepers. They stood at a distance and shouted, "Jesus! Master! Have pity on us!"
    Jesus saw them and said to them, "Go and let the priests examine you."
    On the way they were made clean. One of them, when he saw that he was healed, came back praising God with a loud voice. He threw himself to the ground at Jesus' feet, thanking him. The man was a Samaritan. Jesus spoke up, "There were ten men made clean; where are the other nine? Why is this foreigner the only one who came back to give thanks to God?" And Jesus said to him, "Get up and go; your faith has made you well" (Luke 17:11-19, TEV).

Lastly, it should be pointed out that it was Jesus' radical attitude in breaking down the boundary of scorn against the Samaritan that no doubt caused the author of the Gospel of John to record the story of Jesus' encounter with the Samaritan woman at the well (John 4:3-41). It should be noted that the orthodox* Hebrew would avoid even going through the territory of Samaria, to say nothing of (1) stopping to talk with a Samaritan, (2) who was a woman, and (3) who had a morally questionable reputation.

Yet the whole story of Jesus' compassion for the human being is not complete unless there be added the fact that *his passionate obsession was picking out the scorned, the hurt, the disinherited, and even the so-called undeserving.* It should be said that here is where Jesus steps on modern toes. Today's "nice society" cannot deal with a Jesus like this. Harry Emerson Fosdick wrote: "Outcast, hurt, despised and disreputable folk called out his intense interest and sympathy."[5] He was accused of being a "glutton and a wine bibber." He chose sailors and fishermen as disciples instead of the cream of the universities.

[5] Harry Emerson Fosdick, *The Man from Nazareth* (New York: Harper & Row, Publishers, 1949), p. 131.

In his relentless effort to help the "wretched of the earth," some of his fighting slogans were: "For the Son of man came to seek and to save the lost" (Luke 19:10); "People who are well do not need a doctor, but only those who are sick. Go and find out what this scripture means, 'I do not want animal sacrifices, but kindness.' I have not come to call the respectable people, but the outcasts" (Matthew 9:12-13, TEV); "I have come in order that they might have life, life in all its fulness" (John 10:10, TEV).

No doctrine, tenet, custom, or regulation was to Jesus too sacred to overstep or even discard if it proved to block helping a human being in need. To the utter horror of his fellow Hebrews he once said, "The Sabbath was made for the good of man; man was not made for the Sabbath" (Mark 2:27, TEV).

So then to return to the question with which we began, What made Jesus tick? The answer is that he was obsessed with seeing to it that the creature made in God's image received his or her due in its fullness, without any hindrances, whether such obstructions be from man or the cosmos. His top priority was anybody in need. Need one say more than that Blacks are today the ones most in need?

Jesus' Concept of His Task

In capsule fashion, one could say that Jesus saw his task as being God's agent or ambassador or Messiah for the full liberation of human beings from visible and invisible enslavements. Jesus saw God's will as making the world human, free, and whole. He drew models, images, and thought patterns from his religious heritage to express and explain his sense of divine commission. No doubt he knew of such concepts and categories in his religious tradition, such as "Son of man," "Suffering Servant," and the "Messiah." In ancient Hebrew or Israelite sacred tradition, these titles expressed the conviction that in God's plan for the liberation of his people some kind of divine representative would be forthcoming to bring such to a reality. That hoped-for reality was often referred to as the arrival of the "kingdom of God" or the appearance of the "Day of the Lord." And today, when the term "Jewish messianic hope" is discussed, the reference is to the persistent hope that the Israelites or Hebrews had, particularly after their empires were defeated in 722 and 586 B.C., that God would restore their nation through divine help.

The nature of Hebrew messianic hope went through several modifications. Shortly after the Exile, Hebrews expected their God to raise up a human leader from among them who would possess great religious loyalty and military ability like King David to lead the nation to restoration. This was called the Son of David hope. Later on, the woes of the people became so many and so complex that the belief developed that a mere human being would not be able to secure full liberation. The hope then changed to the expectation that God would send a semi-divine figure from heaven to lead the Hebrews to freedom and greatness. This is called the Son of man hope.

When the conditions of oppression and exploitation became still worse, many Hebrews began to feel that nothing short of a direct intervention of God himself would assure victory over Israel's enemies. This vein of hope is now referred to as apocalyptic* expectation.

Lurking underneath these hopes and expectations always was a strand of thought akin to an element in the covenant faith which was often overshadowed but would not die. This was the belief that Israel's chief God-given role was to serve as God's agent or servant through which God would redeem, humanize, and liberate all other peoples. Through its expression of real human compassion, through its willingness to suffer and sacrifice without vengeance and acrimony, Israel would become the door through which all other nations would come to God and unite in peaceful and productive existence on earth. This was the concept of the "Suffering Servant."

Many biblical scholars now believe that Jesus saw his own mission as fulfilling, with some modifications unique to him, a blending of the Son of man hope and the Suffering Servant concept. Certainly his very strong conviction that he was commissioned by God and his compassion for those who were pushed to the negative fringes of justice, security, and respectability would tend to support this claim. There are those who claim that Jesus of Nazareth did not see himself as playing a messianic role in any sense, but the evidence is too much against that view. And whether Jesus saw himself as the Son of man—Suffering Servant or not, the early church certainly understood him as fulfilling those roles. The evidence is that Jesus did see himself as the expected Son of man (with some modification of popular expectation) and as the Suffering Servant.

It must be remembered that Jesus knew his own Bible (our Old Testament) and the strands of his religious heritage. There are scholars who believe that Jesus brought together the Son of man concept such as that found in Daniel 7:13-18 and the Suffering

Servant concept expressed in Isaiah, chapters 42, 52, and 53.[6] There is great strength for Black liberation in the analysis of these models in Daniel and Second Isaiah. *

Let us analyze the models which these passages reveal. Daniel 7:13-18 reads:

> I saw in the night visions,
> and behold, with the clouds of heaven
> there came one like a son of man,
> and he came to the Ancient of Days
> and was presented before him.
> And to him was given dominion
> and glory and kingdom,
> that all peoples, nations, and languages
> should serve him;
> his dominion is an everlasting dominion,
> which shall not pass away,
> and his kingdom one
> that shall not be destroyed.

"As for me, Daniel, my spirit within me was anxious and the visions of my head alarmed me. I approached one of those who stood there and asked him the truth concerning all this. So he told me, and made known to me the interpretation of the things. *'These four great beasts are the four kings* who shall arise out of the earth. But the *saints of the Most High* shall receive the kingdom, and possess the kingdom for ever, for ever and ever'" (italics added).

In order to understand the passage, it is important to note: (1) The "son of man" here mentioned represents "a people," the "saints," of the Most High as ultimate victors; and (2) the "four beasts" in the passage represent the characteristics of four rulers on earth. Therefore, the thrust of the passage is that a humanizing people or group will eventually rule with justice and equity under God as opposed to the oppressive, "beastly" rulers who have held dominion up to that point. This is God's liberation plan for the earth.

The Son of man will rule like a man (with humanity) in a community committed to God (Most High). He will rule in a manner contrary to the beastly rulers. In his commentary on Daniel 7:13-18, George A. F. Knight states in part: "Since the dominion over *all peoples* given to this son of man by God, in contrast to that seized by the beastly rulers, is to be *everlasting,* the implication is that he is in

---

[6] T. W. Manson, *The Servant-Messiah* (Cambridge, England: Cambridge University Press, 1953), pp. 71-73.

some sense divine. This is suggested at once by his coming *with the clouds of heaven.*"[7]

Knight further writes:

"Saint" is lit. "holy one," translating the same Aramaic word used earlier of angelic beings (4:13, 17, 23; cf. 8:13 in Hebrew); but the reference here is evidently to Israel, called to be a "holy nation" (Exod. 19:6). In ancient Hebrew thought the people of Israel as a whole could be summed up in one representative figure, such as their king, and yet all together they could be called a "son of man" (Ps. 80:17). Thus the meaning here may be that the saints are to receive the kingdom through one who is their representative head, yet in whom they are all included as a kind of corporate personality. He is to be the first real man, in contrast to the past rulers who have been like beasts in spirit (cf. 4:16), and as such institute a kingdom of real men.[8]

There is no doubt that Jesus saw his divinely commissioned role in the sense expressed above. He saw in his own work and initiative an effort which would result in a movement (church) which would serve as a vanguard of the kingdom of God (a society under divine rule consisting of justice, compassion, humility, and liberation). The author of the Gospel of Mark reports Jesus as saying in answer to Pilate's inquiry if he was really the Messiah: "I am, and you will all see the Son of Man seated at the right side of the Almighty, and coming with the clouds of heaven!" (Mark 14:62, TEV).

But Jesus also took upon himself the role of the Suffering Servant expressed in Isaiah chapters 42, 52, 53, and 61. A key passage in chapter 42 is:

> Behold, my servant, whom I uphold,
>   my chosen, in whom my soul delights;
> I have put my Spirit upon him,
>   he will bring forth justice to the nations.
> He will not cry or lift up his voice,
>   or make it heard in the street;
> a bruised reed he will not break,
>   and a dimly burning wick he will not quench;
> he will faithfully bring forth justice (42:1-3).

Note also Isaiah 52:13-15:

> Behold, my servant shall prosper,
>   he shall be exalted and lifted up,
>   and shall be very high.
> As many were astonished at him—

---

[7] *The Interpreter's One-Volume Commentary on the Bible,* p. 445.
[8] *Ibid.,* p. 446.

his appearance was so marred,
   beyond human semblance,
   and his form beyond that of the sons of men—
so shall he startle many nations;
   kings shall shut their mouths because of him;
for that which has not been told them they shall see,
   and that which they have not heard they shall understand.

Every serious student of the Bible has read with fascination this passage which is really a continuation of the servant song in chapter 52:

Who has believed what we have heard?
And to whom has the arm of the Lord been revealed?
For he grew up before him like a young plant,
   and like a root out of dry ground;
he had no form or comeliness that we should look at him,
   and no beauty that we should desire him.
He was despised and rejected by men;
   a man of sorrows, and acquainted with grief;
and as one from whom men hide their faces
   he was despised, and we esteemed him not.

Surely he has borne our griefs
   and carried our sorrows;
yet we esteemed him stricken,
   smitten by God, and afflicted.
But he was wounded for our transgressions,
   he was bruised for our iniquities;
upon him was the chastisement that made us whole,
   and with his stripes we are healed (53:1-5).

Lastly consider Isaiah 61:1-2:

The Spirit of the Lord God is upon me,
Because the Lord has anointed me
   to bring good tidings to the afflicted;
   he has sent me to bind up the brokenhearted,
to proclaim liberty to the captives,
   and the opening of the prison to those who are bound;
to proclaim the year of the Lord's favor.

Now, first note the elements in the servant passages and then scan the New Testament account of Jesus and his ministry and see if there are not similarities. This anointed servant of God avoids a showy limelight. In other words, he is content to stay in the background and not "blow his own horn," so to speak. He is full of compassion for those who are hurt and "unworthy." He will not finish breaking a reed that has been injured or discard a wick which gives off more smoke than light (redemption and rehabilitation rather than vengeance and punishment). He is concerned with justice and liberation with a passion. And he continues to heal and help even when he is injured and rejected in return.

Indeed it seems clear that Jesus early in his ministry had answered through his own experience a question which he is reported to have once raised himself: "Yet why do the Scriptures say that the Son of Man will suffer much and be rejected?" (Mark 9:12, TEV). It may be that Jesus in his own mind made no clear distinction between the Son of man concept and the Suffering Servant idea. Perhaps he earlier came to the conclusion that the corporate (a people) Son of man which would result from his efforts would also be that sacrificing, compassionate, low-profiling group which in the name of justice and liberation would always "go to bat" for the hurt and the needy.

Certainly when one follows the career of Jesus in the Gospels and does the necessary historical and literary research, the influence of these two concepts, Son of man and Suffering Servant—stand out, regardless of whether Jesus saw them as separate or as a blend. Another thing which also seems to stand out is that Jesus' understanding of his divine commission ran counter to much popular messianic hope of his day. Many of his contemporaries expected the Messiah or Son of man to come with extraordinary pomp, egotism, vengeance, military might,[9] and magical powers.

It helps to know this when one reads of such incidents in the Gospels as Jesus' temptations in the wilderness, his ride into Jerusalem on an ass, and his constant refusal to be crowned a king. Popular expectation wanted him to perform the magic of turning stones into bread and jumping off the temple spire without injury. Popular sentiment wanted him to take kingdoms by force and ride into Jerusalem as a victor on a prancing steed rather than on a donkey which symbolized humble means, the poor, the downtrodden. Jesus' rejection of popular expectations was in line with his effort to reverse the value systems into which he was born ("But many who now are first will be last, and many who now are last will be first," Mark 10:31, TEV).

---

[9] R. H. Charles, *The Book of Enoch* (Oxford: Clarendon Press, 1912), pp. 122-125. Note that the Enochian Son of man is very egotistical and bloodthirsty toward Israel's enemies.

Therefore, instead of evaluating a person on the basis of what he or she owns, one will now assess another on how much he or she serves and contributes (Mark 10:41-45). Instead of emphasizing the priorities of "the good" and the privileged, one should concentrate on opening the door for the poor (Luke 4:18) and the disreputable (Mark 2:17; Matthew 11:19). Rather than regarding acts as a test of one's genuineness, Jesus regarded motives (why a person did it) as a true test of character, as is shown in the fifth and sixth chapters of Matthew. In an effort to symbolize his concept of what the Son of man was originally and divinely intended to do and be, Jesus rode into Jerusalem on a donkey instead of a steed, on borrowed garments instead of a glittering saddle, with peasants and pilgrims instead of an army, and with a group which carried palms instead of swords.

This action was a clear reversal of the popular notion of the Son of man modified by the Suffering Servant concept. The temptations in the wilderness represented the popular views. But Jesus saw his divine mission as healing, redeeming, and liberating those who had need of these. It was no afterthought on his part to apply Isaiah 61:1-2 to himself:

> "The Spirit of the Lord is upon me,
>   because he has anointed me to
>   preach good news to the poor.
> He has sent me to proclaim release to the captives,
> and recovering of sight to the blind,
> to set at liberty those who are oppressed,
> to proclaim the acceptable year of the Lord" (Luke 4:18-19).

Jesus' Prophetic Zeal

Walter Rauschenbusch, along with others associated with the so-called "social gospel movement" during the second decade of this century, showed beyond the slightest doubt that Jesus was in line with that strand known as the Hebrew prophetic tradition. That God is Sovereign Judge over heaven and earth (all life) and that persons are the dependent children of God with a right to life with justice divinely granted, Jesus vigorously and passionately affirmed. But under this caption, "Jesus' Prophetic Zeal," the intent is to show that like the Hebrew prophets of the Old Testament, such as Elijah, Amos, Micah, and Nathan, Jesus had the "guts" to "stand up" and "stand out" and "tell it like it was." And he often did so with dripping satire and sarcasm. To tell a group that it strains out gnats but swallows camels is sarcasm at its height. Reminding people that they set aside days to beautify graves of the people they lynched is prophetic satire unparalleled.

It is necessary in our time to see Jesus' prophetic zeal in this sense because of modern mind-sets which paint Jesus as someone who sat in ascetic seclusion withdrawn from controversial issues of the day, and who merely counseled people how to get to heaven. The incident of cleansing the temple (Luke 19:45-46) has already been mentioned. But note that political rulers did not escape Jesus' indignation. In Luke 13:31-32 it is recorded: "At that same time some Pharisees came to Jesus and said to him, 'You must get out of here and go somewhere else, because Herod wants to kill you.' Jesus answered them: 'Go tell that fox: "I am driving out demons and performing cures today and tomorrow, and on the third day I shall finish my work"'" (TEV).

No weak-kneed person in those days called the genocidal maniacs of the Herod family bad names. John the Baptist found that out.

There are two other incidents which speak volumes about Jesus' prophetic courage. One is the refusal to run and hide in the Garden of Gethsemane in spite of great personal agony. The other is his boldness before Pontius Pilate during the trumped-up trial. In later years those reading divinity theology back into these incidents have tended to downgrade Jesus' courage as a human being. Many have said in effect: "Well, since he was the very Son of God, he could afford to be brave, for he could have called on divine intervention to rescue him at any time." But it ought to be remembered that whatever else Jesus was, he was a human being with the same needs, feelings, hopes, and even fears as all of us. He stood as a human being before the dangers and issues of his time.

It is true that those of us who live under the Christian label make the faith affirmation that Jesus was and is unique in God's redeeming and liberating plan. But even we must be willing to affirm that this uniqueness (that which raises Jesus above the rank and file) consists in part in the degree and intensity with which he trusted and obeyed God and with which he loved and worked for the wounded and disinherited of his time.

Jesus and Black Liberation

In dealing with Jesus, the central figure of the New Testament, up to this point, the effort has been to do several things. An attempt was made to show Jesus' continuity with God's liberating covenant plans seen in the Old Testament saga and also to show that in Jesus the covenant plan for liberation was not only continued but also intensified and its victory assured. A second part of the effort was to point out that Jesus was driven by a tremendous sense of justice, compassion, and liberation for human beings, especially those who had been stepped on or left out.

From there the attempt was to go into how Jesus himself saw his God-given purpose in life. We saw that Jesus drew upon models, images, and concepts from his own religious tradition along with his own religious and personal experience for an interpretation of his task. In making use of these concepts, he modified some and intensified others. He regarded himself as fulfilling the roles of the Son of man and the Suffering Servant of Hebraic messianic thought. The former concept was the expectation of a divinely commissioned agent (or a people) who would serve as God's humanizing and liberating instrument among the nations. The latter concept involved a divinely appointed agent (whether singular or corporate is in debate) who would be very compassionate, sacrificial, and nonpunitive in his (their) effort to heal, rehabilitate, bring justice, and liberate.

We are very fortunate in having a record of Jesus using his own Scriptures (Old Testament) to sum up his own view of his task (Isaiah 61:1-2a; Luke 4:16-21). The poor, the "bruised," the enslaved, the brokenhearted—these are the objects of his intense concern.

Lastly, a word was said to dispel the idea that Jesus was a weak-kneed ascetic who was afraid to come down hard on oppressors and tyrants.

Therefore, with the Jesus we now see in the Gospels, it is not too difficult to discern with whom he would stand today were he here in human form. Yet, keep in mind that the New Testament writers maintain that Jesus Christ is essentially still with us. Call it "Holy Spirit," the "Power for liberation," "Divine Influence," or any other label chosen. The One who came to declare "liberty to the captives" and "set the oppressed free" is lined up against a faulty penal system and a slack system of justice in which the majority of those who get arrested, sentenced, jailed, and executed are poor and Black.

Likewise, the One who saw himself as fulfilling the role of a divine figure who refuses to break a "bruised reed" or "quench a dimly burning wick" is working in opposition to those who spend more money and effort on the things of law and order than on justice and rehabilitation. A liberator such as Jesus would exercise whatever effective measures are necessary to see that Black babies do not go to bed hungry in a land of affluence and a nation of plenty where some in power beget mulatto children and prate about "too many welfare mothers"!

A liberator such as Jesus, concerned with "restoring sight to the blind," would see to it that unfortunate and poor Black children attend adequate schools whether they travel on buses or wheelbarrows. The whole busing issue is another of so many dodge games being played in this country.

Pointing to Jesus as liberator, James H. Cone, the Black theologian has written:

> Jesus' work is essentially one of liberation. Becoming a slave himself, he opens realities of human existence formerly closed to man. Through an encounter with Jesus, man now knows the full meaning of God's action in history and man's place within it.
>
> The Gospel of Mark describes the nature of Jesus' ministry in this manner: "The time is fulfilled, the Kingdom of God is at hand; repent and believe the Gospel" (1:14-15). On the face of it, this message appears not to be too radical to our twentieth-century ears, but this impression stems from our failure existentially to bridge the gap between modern man and biblical man. Indeed, the message of the Kingdom strikes at the very center of man's desire to define his own existence in the light of his own interest at the price of his brother's enslavement. It means the irruption of a new age, an age which has to do with God's action in history on behalf of man's salvation. It is an age of liberation, in which "the blind receive their sight, the lame walk, the lepers are cleansed, the deaf hear, the dead are raised up, the poor have the good news preached to them" (Luke 7:22). This is not pious talk, and one does not need a seminary degree to interpret the message. It is a message about the ghetto, and all other injustices done in the name of democracy and religion to further the social, political, and economic interests of the oppressor. In Christ, God enters human affairs and takes sides with the oppressed. Their suffering becomes his, their despair, divine despair. Through Christ the poor man is offered freedom now to rebel against that which makes him other than human.[10]

Black brothers and sisters can count on the presence and liberating power of Jesus the Christ. For "Jesus Christ" is a phrase or term which is attempting to say that the same convictions, attitudes, powers, priorities, and actions which characterized Jesus of Nazareth have been declared by God to be the liberating and redeeming stuff of God's universe.

This is what the apostle Paul meant when, in his astute ability to cut

[10] James H. Cone, *Black Theology and Black Power* (New York: The Seabury Press, Inc., 1969), pp. 35-36.

to the heart of what Jesus was all about, he wrote:

The attitude you should have is the one that Christ Jesus had:

He always had the very nature of God,
but he did not think that by force he should try
to become equal with God.
Instead, of his own free will he gave it all up,
and took the nature of a servant.
He became like man,
and appeared in human likeness;
He was humble and walked the path of obedience to
death—
his death on the cross.
For this reason God raised him to the highest place
above,
and gave him the name that is greater than any other
name,
And so, in honor of the name of Jesus,
all beings in heaven, on earth, and in the
world below
will fall on their knees,
and all will openly proclaim that Jesus Christ is
the Lord,
to the glory of God the Father (Philippians 2:5-11, TEV).

One must not mistake the testimony of Black church members who cry out: "I walked with Jesus this morning!" They are not talking about walking with some visible figure down the sidewalk. They are attempting to put into words the fact that they were caught up in meditation on and genuine communion with that same liberating, sustaining, living, and directing presence which made Jesus the capstone of God's freedom plan. Black brothers and sisters should continue to embrace the biblical faith which in its Jesus-centeredness has been the underpinning of the Black American religious experience. It is this faith of being in cadence with Jesus that has helped Blacks in America affirm that they were indeed sons and daughters of God. In fact, those who sensed that God through Jesus held the downtrodden to be his special priority have declared that Blacks in America are special sons of God. A Black deacon was heard to proclaim in a devotional service: "They can't close the gates until I get there! Praise His Holy name!"

But to those who ask for a demonstration of the Jesus power or the Liberating Spirit, two things must be said. The first is that in spite of the fact that Black liberation (and ultimately all liberation) is the divine wave of the future, God calls for human participation in and cooperation with his divine liberation activity before liberation *de jure* becomes liberation *de facto*. This is indeed the nature of the covenant, it will be recalled. God refuses to liberate unilaterally. Liberation occurs when the power of God and the action of the people meet. Jesus never called on God to send a legion of angels to fly him into Jerusalem or to whisk him away from Gethsemane.

The second thing to be pointed out is that the Jesus liberating power had been and is manifested in our midst. Thousands of Black and white church members (orthodox and nonorthodox) took stands against racial injustice. This fact is not made less by the legitimate feeling that there could have been more.

Moreover, the Jesus power is seen in such Black economic cooperative efforts as Leon Sullivan's O.I.C., Jesse Jackson's Operation P.U.S.H., and such activities as those sponsored by Vincent Harding, Albert Cleage, Andrew Young, and Ralph Abernathy. The liberating power has been experienced in the hundreds of Black congregations and communities throughout the country which never make headlines but which serve day after day as centers of Black cohesion, wholeness, healing, and direction.

God's power is operating in Black political action efforts, in Black college support, in youth rebellions against social evils, such as the sit-ins and the freedom rides. The power of Jesus even made itself known in economic boycotts and selective buying efforts, in voter-registration seminars. Wherever there were and are genuine efforts to free men and women, there is the liberating power of Jesus. And, it may be added, the very dissatisfaction which Black people now feel as they make their protest against all forms of injustice is the result of the Jesus power which will not allow them to be apathetic in face of social wrongs.

Freedom emerges wherever and whenever a people actively moves with Jesus on the liberation trail. For "if the Son makes you free, you will be free indeed" (John 8:36).

Gospel Points Aiding Black Liberation

While there is little reference to race or color in the gospel, as these distinctions are known to us today, Black Americans can identify with certain stances and insights in the Gospels attributed either to Jesus or to God through Jesus' attitudes and activities. Such identification is of course made possible by several facts.

The first is that the Gospels were written by and for the early church, which consisted of a persecuted and hounded people. The Black American can therefore sense a kinship with such a group. The second fact is that the Gospels are faith writings directing the persecuted and the hopeless to center their trust and hope in a redeeming and liberating God who would, with the people's response, make liberation happen in a manner and with a power not expected by the world. American Blacks today in a sense look to the God of history to make the seemingly impossible a liberated reality.

Here space will not permit the quotation of each passage to support the stance. The reader is invited to check the references. Some of the material which will be noted has been alluded to previously.

The Gospel of Mark

The Gospel of Mark was written around A.D. 70, to a martyr church whose members often had to read it by candlelight in the catacombs (hollow cemeteries). The following points it stresses are relevant to Black liberation:

1. Jesus announced the nearness of the kingdom of God and the need for all to repent in preparation for receiving it. Scholarship shows that the term meant a type of earthly society in which God is acknowledged as King in terms of justice, compassion, and humility (1:14-15).
2. Jesus' priority was ministering to human needs in contrast to performing religious rituals (chapters 2 and 3).
3. Jesus extolled contribution to the well-being of the human family rather than acquisition from it (10:35-45).
4. Jesus criticized charlatans who exploited the helpless (12:38-40) and those who said the right things for the wrong reasons (14:3-9).
5. Jesus declared the equality and liberation of women (10:2-12).
6. Jesus led a demonstration to protest false notions of the messianic hope (11:1-10).
7. Jesus expressed his passionate indignation at the exploitation and cheating of poor and unwitting pilgrims at the temple market (11:15-19).

The Gospel of Luke

The Gospel of Luke, written by a physician of that name, A.D. 90, stresses points in Jesus' ministry which would appeal to one

concerned with human misery and the tragic in human life, namely:
1. Jesus' temptations (4:1-13).
2. Jesus affirmed that apathy in face of God's will is blasphemous (6:46-49).
3. Jesus shattered the barrier of ethnic prejudice (7:1-9) and the "pure blood" boundary (10:25-37; 17:11-19).
4. Jesus condemned selfishness and selfcenteredness (12:13-21).
5. Jesus affirmed that God's priority always rests with those in need (19:10; 15:3-32).

The Gospel of Matthew

The Gospel of Matthew was written sometime after Mark, perhaps around A.D. 80-85, by an author who either was a Hebrew (or Jew) or who knew well Jewish history and tradition, for he was convinced that Jesus was the Messiah long awaited by the Jewish people. The author believed that Jesus fulfilled and clarified many elements of the Jewish historical covenant tradition and made other elements unnecessary because he was God's final and complete revelation. This author also believed that, in Jesus, God had initiated universal access to his grace as the covenant faith said he would. Here are some of his points regarding Jesus:
1. Jesus insisted that there was no true obedience to God without reconciliation of broken human relations, and that no time should be lost in securing reconciliation lest the relations fester (5:23-26).
2. Jesus affirmed that mere rhetoric carried no premium with God (7:21-23).
3. Jesus taught that God's priority is helping the needy (9:12-13; 25:31-46).

The Gospel of John

The author of the Gospel of John (unknown) was more concerned with writing a theological interpretation of the facts surrounding Jesus' ministry. This Gospel was written much later than the other three, around A.D. 115, to fill a need for non-Jewish Christians of Graeco-Roman origin.

The author of this Gospel had three main aims in mind: (1) He wrote to show that Jesus was the Christ or Messiah expected by the Hebrews, yet important to the whole human race. (2) He wanted to refute those who formed a "John cult" that claimed John the Baptist, not Jesus, was the Messiah. (3) He opposed the Gnostics who claimed that only an elite group could attain divinity through right knowledge and ritual and that God would not visit the human realm in any incarnation because the human realm was inherently evil.

The following points in John throw light on the task of Black liberation:

1. Jesus Christ shows that God is acting against those world-renouncing philosophies which claim that the gospel should not be applied to the social order (1:1-14).
2. God as reflected in Jesus Christ loves his world and is acting to redeem and liberate it (3:16-17).
3. Jesus Christ reaches over ethnic barriers (4:5-40).
4. Under God martyrdom for the cause of liberation actually aids rather than hinders the progress of liberation (12:23-26).
5. Monuments to those murdered cannot erase the guilt and responsibility shared by those who violate human rights and human dignity (19:6-22).

Apostle Paul and the Black American

We are faced with a disturbing irony in the Black communities, an irony which stems from the fact that the greatest spokesman for the early Christian movement and its most prolific writer (at least eleven documents preserved) is now the object of suspicion and doubt in the minds of many Black Americans. This man is the apostle Paul.

This is not the first time that this man who has influenced theological thought from the North African Augustine to the reformer Martin Luther to Karl Barth and Reinhold Niebuhr of our day has been under suspicion. Nineteenth-century German theological scholarship accused Paul of subverting the Jesus of history in favor of the Christ of faith. Later all of us had to admit that, as long as we had human beings whose faith affirmed and interpreted Jesus as the Christ, we would inescapably have a Christ of faith.

But Black suspicion of Paul is so strong that some claim that he diluted a Black liberation movement (early Christian movement) started by a Black man (Jesus) by injecting into it White, Graeco-Roman thought. A second charge they make against Paul is that he favored human slavery, or at least he did little to uproot it. The Reverend Albert Cleage's work, *The Black Messiah,* is an example of such charges.

This writer does not agree with these charges. In the first place, historical research does not support the charge that Paul either favored or was indifferent to the then well-established and generally accepted institution of human slavery of his day. Hard scholarship overwhelmingly tends to show that Paul was ahead of his own time in sensing that there was something deeply demonic about human slavery. Scholarship further shows that Paul was the purest representative that the early church produced of what Jesus originally espoused. Who can forget the rows he had with Simon Peter and the Jerusalem group over their prejudice against Gentiles? It was really Paul who first saw and proclaimed the universal nature of the gospel. It is nothing short of a miracle that he discerned that in Christ there is neither Jew nor Greek, wise nor unwise, bond nor free, male nor female, but Christ being the center for all radiating across all man-made boundaries.

Some of the questions about Paul were discussed in chapter 1, but some repetition may be necessary here. It is historically irresponsible and academically callous to hurl twentieth-century moral and theological judgments against a churchman of the first century without first noting certain historically conditioned facts shaping his theology.

First, to ignore the fact that Paul gave much of his advice in the perspective of his belief that the Second Coming was just days away is to do him a grave injustice. When Paul advised people against wedding preparations and divorce proceedings, he was not speaking from some theological ban against women or marriage. He actually believed that there was not enough time even to finish such plans. When he counseled that persons should remain in whatever condition that prevailed when they were "called," he was not telling people to bear social ills stoicly. He was saying that time was so short that it would make little difference, for Jesus Christ would soon clear the old order anyway.

Twentieth-century critics can make a case against Paul for having bad eschatology (a doctrine of God's final consummation), but they can hardly support the claim that he was morally or theologically indifferent to human misery.

Although Paul was a busy, traveling evangelist and not a systematic theologian, he possessed a solid guiding conviction: whoever is really "in Christ" is a transformed person whose attitudes, desires, outlooks, and goals are lifted to a higher level. He believed that this fact alone guaranteed transformation of the whole of God's order. Paul's modern critics, who claim that Paul diluted Jesus, have not yet shown wherein Paul's central conviction conflicts with Jesus' central invitation to repent and be reborn in preparation for the kingdom of God.

A good example of how Paul expected the transforming power of being in league with Jesus to change the social fabric is seen in Paul's letter to Philemon. Here the evangelist was writing to a slaveholding deacon in the church about the deacon's runaway slave. This slave was the deacon's property under the law, a legal concept just as secure then as the one which allows a twentieth-century American to own a home. The slave had stolen some property as he left. Later the slave, Onesimus, ran into Paul on his escape route and confessed that he was a fugitive. Paul had several options open to him.

A callous and insensitive law-and-order person would have had the slave locked up and his owner notified. That was the obviously legal thing to do. Still Paul could have taken the pious stand of persuading Onesimus to return and "take his medicine," with, of course, the promise that Paul would pray for him. Or there may be those who feel that Paul should have counseled him to "keep running." But where would he run in the Roman Empire and forever evade captors? The truth is that the short life span of a fugitive was in front of him, and sure death was behind him.

What did the Apostle do? He sent Onesimus back with a fellow apostle bearing a covering letter in which Paul threw the full force of his moral and ecclesiological authority behind the well-being of this young man. One must remember that runaway slaves received as punishment at the least disfigurement (loss of a hand, a leg, the eyes, or the tongue) and execution at the most, especially if theft were involved.

Paul, with alternating persuasion and command, asked Philemon, the deacon, to receive Onesimus as if he were the apostle himself. He further asked in mock fashion that Philemon charge him for any thefts which Onesimus committed. And in addition to affirming that Onesimus was a "brother in Christ," Paul threatened to visit Philemon after his (Paul's) release from prison to see if Philemon had carried out his wish.

This just does not seem like the action of a man who was insensitive to slavery or who had misinterpreted Jesus. Blacks, of all people in this day and time, should cease to rely on secondhand opinion making and instead research for themselves the basis of their own thinking and beliefs. Without the work of the apostle Paul, the New Testament would be weak indeed.

For here is an early Christian spokesman who can admonish and edify Blacks that, as Jesus taught in his parable of the prodigal sons, *agape* (God's kind of love) does not quit or give up on brothers and sisters who are down; that God's kind of love will remove the greed that makes one get fat off his brother's poverty and misery; that God's kind of love makes a brother stand up for right and come down hard on wrong. This love clears away grudges, big I's and little you's, and childish bickering. The Black community must hear the Apostle.

Questions for Further Study

1. What periods can you identify in the history of the Black American when, as in the days of the early church, the loss of the fear of pain and death produced liberating results?
2. How did Jesus himself see his own mission on earth?
3. Why does James Cone call Jesus *"the* Liberator"?
4. What is the real picture of Jesus offered in the Gospels?
5. Can the assertion that Paul radically deviated from Jesus' call for liberation and transformation really be sustained? Why or why not?

For Additional Reading

Fosdick, Harry Emerson, *Jesus of Nazareth* (New York: Random House, Inc., 1959).

_____, *The Man from Nazareth* (New York: Harper & Row, Publishers, 1949).

The Interpreter's One-Volume Commentary on the Bible, Treatments of Mark and Luke (Nashville: Abingdon Press, 1971).

Phillips, J. B., *Letters to Young Churches* (New York: The Macmillan Company, 1958).

Rall, Harris Franklin, *According to Paul* (New York: Charles Scribner's Sons, 1950).

Rauschenbusch, Walter, *The Social Principles of Jesus* (Philadelphia: The American Baptist Publication Society, 1916).

Bible Concepts Needing Reexamination for the Black Struggle

4

A "concept" is an idea structure giving guidance to a point of view or an action. But, like words and terms, a concept can become old and stale. When it does, it becomes not only useless but also can even get in the way of fresh thought and can muddy clear thinking. Sometimes a worn-out concept can pick up meanings which were never a part of the original idea. This is why people must be on their guard and constantly reexamine concepts.

There are concepts which have developed in connection with the Bible and the Christian faith which should be reexamined to see if they still say and mean what the Bible, rightly understood, is saying and meaning. Often people are heard to say: "The Good Book says that dancing is a sin," or "The Bible says that women who wear slacks will not go to heaven," or "God said in the Bible that the church shouldn't have anything to do with political, economic, and social matters." Often such people are not aware of what the Bible really teaches on such matters or even if the Bible touches on these matters at all.

Let us look at some concepts which need reexamination in light of the biblical faith and Black liberation.

The Concept of Sin

The Bible throughout deals with the concept of sin. It teaches that sin is our central human problem, the cause of separation between God and us and between person and person. It seems from this biblical tradition that people early wondered about the cause of human moral and ethical imperfections, of human conflicts and hostilities, and of human disrespect for the Divine.

But if sin is simply sin for everybody, Black or White, why bother to discuss it in the context of Black liberation? It is true that "sin" in the truly biblical sense of the term does apply to all. But a live question circulating in many Black communities today is whether or not the biblical concept of sin has been distorted to some degree by White religion and, like so many other things, shaped into a tool for Black derogation and control? A twin question is: Has the White religious community in some areas of the country, if not all, diluted the biblical concept of sin into a catalog of petty, individual sins to blunt their guilt for grand sins committed against Blacks?

Let us take a look at the biblical concept of sin and see if there is any truth to these charges. The bibical tradition opens with an attempt to deal with sin in the early chapters of the book of Genesis. In Genesis 2:16-17 it is written: "And the Lord God commanded the man, saying, 'You may freely eat of every tree of the garden; but of the tree of the knowledge of good and evil you shall not eat, for in the day that you eat of it you shall die.'"

In Genesis 3:1-7, we find this passage:

Now the serpent was more subtle than any other wild creature that the Lord God had made. He said to the woman, "Did God say, 'You shall not eat of any tree of the garden'?" And the woman said to the serpent, "We may eat of the fruit of the trees of the garden; but God said, 'You shall not eat of the fruit of the tree which is in the midst of the garden, neither shall you touch it, lest you die.'" But the serpent said to the woman, "You will not die. For God knows that when you eat of it your eyes will be opened, and you will be like God, knowing good and evil." So when the woman saw that the tree was good for food, and that it was a delight to the eyes, and that the tree was to be desired to make one wise, she took of its fruit and ate; and she also gave some to her husband, and he ate. Then the eyes of both were opened, and they knew that they were naked; and they sewed fig leaves together and made themselves aprons.

For centuries both Jews and Christians, in their effort to explain and understand the mystery, power, deadliness, and the universality of the evil influence of sin, have wrestled with these two passages.

From these is extracted the doctrine traditionally called the "Fall of Man." Under biblical exegesis and scholarship what do these passages give us in terms of explaining sin?

St. Augustine, the early African church giant, using these passages in his exposition on sin wrote:

> But evil began within them secretly at first, to draw them into open disobedience afterwards. For there would have been no evil work, but there was an evil will before it: and what could begin this evil will but pride, that is the beginning of all sin? And what is pride but a perverse desire of height, in forsaking Him to whom the soul ought solely to cleave, as the beginning thereof, to make the self seem the one beginning.[1]

Note here that Augustine is using the term "pride" not in the sense of that which causes a young man to wash his socks. What Augustine (and Luther, Calvin, and R. Niebuhr) meant by the term is the urge to displace God and play his role. This is the taproot of sin.

Albert T. Rasmussen wrote:"There is in all of us a sinful pride to want to be better than others and to enforce our superiority over those whom we want to keep inferior for our own advantage."[2]

No doubt a similar insight prompted James H. Cone to write:

> But through sin man rejects his proper activity and destiny. He wants to be God, the creator of his destiny. This is the essence of sin, every man's desire to become "like God." But in his passion to become super-human, man becomes subhuman, estranged from the source of his being, threatening and threatened by his neighbor, transforming a situation destined for intimate human fellowship into a spider web of conspiracy and violence.[3]

The direction toward a definition of the biblical concept of sin is clear. The chief root of sin is the attempt on the part of the human creature to play God. Genesis 3:5 is central, for it seems to imply motive: "for God doth know that in the day ye eat thereof, then your eyes shall be opened, and ye shall be as God [gods], knowing good and evil." According to the Jewish scholar commenting on this verse in *The Pentateuch and Haftorahs: "as God* [means] you will become endowed with a power which is at present reserved exclusively to Himself, *viz.* omniscience (Sforno); and, having acquired omniscience, you will be in a position to repudiate His authority."[4]

[1] St. Augustine, *City of God,* pp. 29-30 (Book 12, Chapter 13).
[2] Albert T. Rasmussen, *Christian Social Ethics* (Englewood Cliffs, N.J.: Prentice Hall, Inc., 1956), p. 236.
[3] James H. Cone, *Black Theology and Black Power* (New York: The Seabury Press, Inc., 1969), p. 63.
[4] J. H. Hertz, ed., *The Pentateuch and Haftorahs* (London: Soncino Press, 5722–1962), p. 10.

The true biblical concept of sin with a capital S is that kind of self-centered, promethian* defiance of God which in turn causes one to be a law unto oneself and to attempt to dominate and exploit and injure one's neighbor. It is essential for Blacks to know this not only because they have been the victims of Whites' attempts to play God in America, but also because the biblical concept of sin has often been corrupted by the earlier master-slave relationships and the subsequent relationships in which Whites have been favored and Blacks disfavored.

The concept was filtered through White interpretation and vested interest. Whatever favored White advantage became "good," and whatever tended toward Black advantage, Black freedom, and rebellion became a "sin." Gayraud Wilmore in his discussion of Martin R. Delany, the Black lay theologian (1812-1855), writes:

> His problem with religion in the Black community was that the Black churches, imitating the pietism of nineteenth-century Protestant evangelicalism, were giving Negroes the impression that the reason for their miserable condition was their immorality and that what was required for salvation was "being good."[5]

Now this "being good" consisted in "not stealing the master's goods," not contributing to slave rebellions, obeying the overseer's orders, being polite to Whites, working hard, and reporting "suspicious" activities of other Blacks. In the days after Emancipation the catalog of sins dictated by the White power structure and many Black churches consisted of a ban against alcohol, sexual activity, frolics, gambling, and riling the tempers of Whites.

These regulations safeguarded White advantage, for they assured sober work crews, the sexual security of White women, fewer problems for law enforcement on weekends, and a generally docile Black population.

The whole point of the matter is that the string of petty sins formed another mental chain around the minds of Blacks while White folk committed the big sin by biblical standards—that of playing God by dominating, exploiting, and injuring Black folk. This is not a plea for Blacks to become immoral, but it is a caution against Blacks allowing themselves to share more guilt in their everyday living than they deserve and thus becoming spiritually and mentally debilitated in their struggle for freedom. In spite of the efforts to get them to think

[5] Gayraud S. Wilmore, *Black Religion and Black Radicalism* (Garden City: Doubleday & Company, Inc., 1972), pp. 151-152.

so, they are not the worst creatures on the globe. For the big sin is and always was dehumanizing, destroying, and undermining one's brothers and sisters.

The Concept That Being a Christian Is Between the Person and God Alone

"We are doing all right, just my God and I" are the opening words of an old congregational song which was popular years ago in Southern Black congregations. It was "spirited," but it was not Christian. For the true Christian faith does not teach that following Jesus Christ is strictly a "private affair." Rather, it teaches that along with one's devotional life *must* go a proper relationship with one's neighbor. The two must hang together, and each must blend in with and receive strength from the other. Christian commitment is social as well as private. It involves ethics (right acts toward one's neighbor) as well as personal devotion (prayer and ritual).

The fact of the matter is that Jesus himself, being an heir of the Israelite prophets, pointed out that right relations with one's brother (or sister) should precede devotional acts. In Matthew 5:23-24, it is reported that he said: "So if you are about to offer your gift to God at the altar and there you remember that your brother has something against you, leave your gift there in front of the altar and go at once to make peace with your brother; then come back and offer your gift to God" (TEV).

Jesus, as an heir of the Israelite prophets, would have been well aware of their insistence that the covenant faith carried the demand for ethical righteousness (treating other people with justice and compassion) as well as the demand for personal allegiance to God or religious observance. The great "Social Gospel" sage, Walter Rauschenbusch, lamenting that American Christianity never took seriously enough its prophetic roots, wrote:

> The prophets were the heralds of the fundamental truth that religion and ethics are inseparable, and that ethical conduct is the supreme and sufficient religious act. If that principle had been fully adopted in our religious life, it would have turned the full force of the religious impulse into the creation of right moral conduct and would have made the unchecked growth and accumulation of injustice impossible.[6]

Black people must sense that what the indictment by Rauschen-

[6] Walter Rauschenbusch, *Christianity and the Social Crisis* (New York: The Macmillan Company, 1907), p. 7.

busch and others means is that American Christianity as a whole never took prophetic religion and Jesus of Nazareth seriously. Many church folk shied away from actively opposing social wrongs. This allowed social and economic injustice to increase, as Blacks very well know.

It will be remembered that when the question arose in this country as to whether a Black slave who was converted would be given his or her freedom as a result, the answer was "no" because, it was argued, the slave's "inward" status had nothing to do with his or her "outward" status. Here was an opportunity lost forever to affirm the full prophetic nature of the gospel. Kenneth M. Stampp wryly observed: "When the first Africans were imported in the seventeenth century, some purchasers opposed converting them to Christianity lest baptism give them a claim to freedom. After the colonial legislatures provided that conversion would not have this effect, the opposition diminished."[7]

American Christianity as a whole then drifted in the direction of "soul saving" and creating congregations of private morality and personal devotion. With this emphasis, concern for social and corporate righteousness faded. This is why Hayward Henry, Jr., describing White laymen as a whole, could write: "Basically they want their church to tend to the private religious needs of its members and to stay out of such questions as peace, social justice, and human rights."[8]

Let Black people be aware that "soul only," private, society-ducking religion is not Christian and prophetic. It is not biblical. The Bible affirms that God is in the business of liberating the whole person—in the inward and outward condition, in the private and social contest. The biblical and Christian mandate always is: "I was hungry and you fed me, thirsty and you gave me drink; I was a stranger and you received me in your homes, naked and you clothed me; I was sick and you took care of me, in prison and you visited me" (Matthew 25:35-36, TEV).

True Christianity is never "my God and I" in exclusion; it is "our God and we." It is enlightening to hear Afro-American and African scholars discuss African social philosophy and religion, for they

[7] Kenneth M. Stampp, "To Make Them Stand in Fear," *The Black Church in America,* ed. Hart M. Nelsen, *et al.* (New York: Basic Books, Inc., Publishers, 1971), p. 54.

[8] Hayward Henry, Jr., "Toward a Religion of Revolution," *The Black Scholar,* December, 1970, p. 28.

point out that communality (social oneness) and ontological monism (the whole of life is interlocking—nature, persons, the spirit world, etc.) are the basic elements in African thought. This viewpoint is closer to biblical faith than we previously realized. For the Bible heavily affirms our corporate responsibility under God.

The Concept That the Bible Affirms World Abandonment

Often one hears that the Bible teaches that a person must withdraw from involvement in the world and wait to be rescued from it by God in the Second Coming. Shallow reading of the Bible and a lazy spirit have been responsible for the adoption of this point of view. The Bible does not teach that God regards his world as something alien or something to be escaped and destroyed.

Even the very books of the Bible so much misused by people of the abandonment persuasion affirm God's rule on earth rather than away from it (Daniel and Revelation). The Book of Daniel affirms that God in his sovereignty operates in the affairs of people and nations. The book of Revelation has New Jerusalem "coming down" to earth where God will abide with his people. Also it is interesting to note that even many of the extreme millenarian* groups are now predicting that there will be a divine rule on earth in some form. The notion that God will destroy his physical cosmos by "fire" has been greatly modified, and many Christians now suspect that the term "fire" in biblical context symbolically denotes purification rather than literally meaning destruction.

But even more significant has been the appearance of a host of solid scholars[9] looking at the biblical faith and society over the last thirteen years. These scholars and their works have had a tremendous impact on Christian thought along the line of reaffirming God's concern for his world as the very arena of God's action and cooperative human

[9] Harvey Cox, *The Secular City* (New York: The Macmillan Company, 1966).

Harvey Cox, *God's Revolution and Man's Responsibility* (Valley Forge: Judson Press, 1965).

Colin Williams, *Where in the World?* (New York: National Council of the Churches of Christ, 1963; *What in the World?* (Epworth Press, 1965).

Peter L. Berger, *The Noise of Solemn Assemblies* (New York: Doubleday & Company, Inc., 1961).

Gibson Winter, *The Suburban Captivity of the Churches* (New York: The Macmillan Company, 1962).

Robert A. Raines, *New Life in the Church* (New York: Harper & Row, Publishers, 1961).

Gayraud Wilmore, *The Secular Relevance of the Church* (Philadelphia: The Westminster Press, 1962).

response. Separately and together these scholars have affirmed the following: (1) The gap between what we so long called "secular" activities and "sacred" work must be erased, for the whole world and all activity come under God; (2) the God of the Bible, the prophets, the covenant, and of Jesus Christ declares his creation to be "good"; (3) the church must deliberately take its work into the world, the area of God's liberating and saving activity; and (4) the church is to recognize that it is the active servant and divine instrument of the kingdom of God and not the kingdom itself.

Persons who attempt to find biblical support for the concept of world abandonment have to explain away passages such as the following. The author of the Gospel of John wrote: "For God loved the world so much that he gave his only Son, so that everyone who believes in him may not die but have eternal life" (3:16, TEV). The author of Revelation wrote: "Then the seventh angel blew his trumpet, and there were loud voices in heaven, saying, 'The power to rule over the world belongs now to our Lord and his Messiah, and he will rule forever and ever!'" (11:15, TEV).

On the question of how God regards his creation, the author of Genesis represents God as declaring his creation to be good. Note Genesis 1:10: "And God saw that it was good"; and in verses 12, 18, 21, 25 there is the same affirmation. In verse 31 we read: "And God saw everything that he had made, and behold, it was very good."

In the discussion of the New Testament we noted that the author of the Gospel of John had as one of his main aims the contradiction of the Gnostics, a group who affirmed a kind of world abandonment. His statement that the "Word was made flesh" was really a slap at the Gnostics. Here is what that author wrote as a report of Jesus' prayer: "I do not ask you to take them out of the world, but I do ask you to keep them safe from the Evil One" (17:15, TEV). Here Jesus was praying for his followers "in the world."

Why is the destruction of the "world-abandonment" notion so important to the Black struggle for liberation? One answer is that the same type of mind-set which says that the world is evil, that God cares nothing for it, that the church should not get involved in the world's ills is the mind-set which usually hates civil rights for Blacks, the United Nations, the World Council of Churches, a multifaith society, and the labor movement. But, perhaps more importantly, it is the same mind-set that can lynch a Black man on Saturday afternoon and receive Communion on the following Sunday morning because of the dichotomy it has drawn between "heaven and earth" or religion and the "world."

Another reason it is important for Blacks to beware of this abandonment philosophy is that it counsels Blacks to withdraw from the effort to secure liberation "here and now" and "cop-out." For, if a Black mind can be made to accept the belief that the world is evil and hated by God himself, then such a mind will exert no effort to improve the world.

It is past the time when Black people must affirm liberation in this world here and now. They must affirm that this is God's world, that they are God's people, and that God wants them to enjoy the world which he has made.

The Concept of the Kingdom: Locational, Chronological, or Responsive

Scholars are certainly correct when they say that the concept of the kingdom of God (or kingdom of heaven) is central to the major proclamation and ministry of Jesus. The Gospel of Mark (the oldest Gospel) pictures Jesus as beginning his ministry with the proclamation: "The right time has come, and the Kingdom of God is near! Turn away from your sins and believe the Good News!" (1:15, TEV). In his prayer instructions, Jesus taught his followers to pray: "May your Kingdom come; may your will be done on earth as it is in heaven" (Matthew 6:10, TEV).

Biblical scholars are also right when they teach that the kingdom concept is rooted in Hebrew thought and history as part of the "Day of the Lord" idea and represents a hope for an earthly society in which God would be acknowledged as King in terms of a manifestation of justice, compassion, and humility. Therefore, Jesus was not introducing a concept alien to his fellow Jews. What was new in his proclamation was that he declared that in the event represented by his appearance, his activity, his person, and his movement the kingdom of God was breaking into the human scene, was becoming a reality to which people must respond.

But modern confusion surrounding the concept has come mainly from two quarters. One source of confusion has been that too many lay people have overspiritualized the "kingdom of God" to mean "where good people go when they pass away." The notion that Jesus envisioned the kingdom as an earthly realization wherever and whenever people actively responded to God's power and will faded into the background. The kingdom became that "glorious realm beyond this vale of tears."

The other source of befuddlement can be laid at the door of some biblical scholars who, with all of their honest, hard work, buried the concept in theoretical speculation. They raised such questions as these: What is the nature of the kingdom, inward attitude or outward manifestation? Where and when is it to be found, here and now or in the future beyond history?

Even beautiful, theoretical statements have for decades been written about the presence of the kingdom without satisfying the hunger of liberation-minded Blacks in America. From the standpoint of the Black agenda these neat questions fail to get to the crux of concrete results, which will make a real difference in the conditions of Black people. In face of beautiful theological jargon, some Blacks are asking if this is not another case of talking to keep from doing, or of delivering a sermon to drown out the cries for bread, for essays on the kingdom do little toward pinpointing and promising concrete results in terms of Black liberation.

The research and scholarship of these writers were notable, to be sure, but the Black American who searched through them often felt that he saw the weeds shaking without even being able to see the deer, so to speak. For instance, Morton Scott Enslin wrote:

> His message was simple. Mark summarizes it: "The time is fulfilled, and the kingdom of God is at hand: repent ye and believe in the gospel;" that is, believe that this good news that the Father's greatest gift to men is at hand is true. It can scarcely be doubted that he sounded his message with the full confidence that the nation would harken and rejoice. It was all so clear to him; nothing else in life mattered. The Father had spoken. Of course God's children would obey as soon as they heard his voice.[10]

But many "children" did not and do not hear his voice, and many Black children have not experienced the liberation of the kingdom. Again, said Frederick C. Grant:

> The theological significance of the opening words of Mark 1:14 is clear: the imprisonment of John is the signal for Jesus' return to Galilee; the clause "the time is fulfilled" (unless it is textually secondary) probably does not refer to the onward march of the aeons, as it would in apocalyptic, but to the current event of John's arrest. John had been the preacher of judgment to come; his arrest marks the beginning of the end. Hence Jesus begins at once his preaching of "the gospel of the kingdom of God" (which is

[10] Morton Scott Enslin, *Christian Beginnings* (New York: Harper & Row, Publishers, 1938), p. 158.

probably the true reading). Like John, Jesus sets repentance in the forefront of his message, but the rest is different—whereas John had threatened his hearers with the impending doom of the Last Judgment, Jesus is the preacher of the "glad tidings" of God's reign.[11]

Here again, what does "God's reign" mean in terms of concrete results touching justice and liberation for Black Americans? Is Grant's statement any more than theological theory? Does it have any meaning in the existential Black situation? The same questions can be asked of towering scholars like C. H. Dodd and T. W. Manson. Manson wrote in his celebrated work:

> To sum up. The kingdom of God is *God's* kingdom, *God's* reign. That is, it is the actualisation in history of God's power and wisdom as the secret of all true human welfare. The Israelite ideal is a God-given standard. The basic claim of the Gospel is that in Jesus the kingdom of God has come to Israel, the Israelites' God-given ideal is realised.[12]

True, the kingdom of God may have come to Israel, but has it come to the Black ghettos in Chicago and New York City? Is this not a case of talking about yesteryear to avoid today's demands?

Even C. H. Dodd, who seemed to sense that scholarship on the kingdom of God tended to dwell either in the past or in the future, stopped short of clarifying how one recognized or realized concrete present results of the kingdom vis-à-vis the Western world's greatest issue, racial justice. He does a real service to New Testament scholarship when he writes: "Whatever we make of them, the sayings which declare the Kingdom of God to have come are explicit and unequivocal. They are moreover the most characteristic and distinctive of the Gospel sayings on the subject."[13] Nevertheless, Dodd does little more than other scholars in showing where the present power of the kingdom can be seen to operate.

Before the discourse is continued, three things ought to be said as to why the kind of speculation about the kingdom earlier described was doomed to failure from the start. First, the whole debate as to whether the kingdom of God was present (realized) or future (eschatological) kept the concept suspended in limbo and thus allowed many White church people to avoid consciously or

[11] Frederick C. Grant, *An Introduction to New Testament Thought* (New York: Abingdon Press, 1950), p. 212.
[12] T. W. Manson, *The Servant-Messiah* (Cambridge, England: Cambridge University Press, 1953), p. 74.
[13] C. H. Dodd, *Parables of the Kingdom* (New York: Charles Scribner's Sons, 1936), p. 49.

unconsciously the hard demand to rid the present world of its social ills.

Secondly, the debate on where and when the kingdom is to be located betrayed some biblical amnesia on the part of scholars who forgot that the unifying and central thread of the biblical faith is the covenant between God and his people. The nature of the covenant is a two-way street, so to speak. In it, God is present with the pledge of *liberating power* and *direction,* and the people are alertly present with the pledge of *total allegiance* and *active obedience.* Liberation, the fruit of the kingdom, is the result of a cooperative venture between God and his people.

Lastly, the kingdom of God is not primarily an object to be passively located in some particular place at some particular time. Neither is it something created by men and women alone or served up by God alone. Its reality is the result of the call-and-response covenant between God and the people. It is wherever and whenever the power and potential of God meet the obedient action of a people. From God's side, the kingdom is made available, from the people's side, the kingdom is something actively harvested. Depending on the motive of the speaker, to say that God helps those who help themselves can be solid covenant theology. As long as the motive behind the assertion is not to avoid "helping the brother down under," it is good to remember that God operates through a people's commitment and action.

Robert A. Bennett has reminded us that "it is not only by the mighty acts of God himself, as at the exodus and conquest and in Jesus' life and resurrection, but also by human response to these divine motions that the model for society is forged." [14] There is too much of the wrong kind of "waiting on God." Gayraud S. Wilmore states that Martin R. Delany used to maintain that "a spiritual blessing is to be prayed for, a moral good sought by exercising one's sense of justice, and a physical end requires the use of might and muscle." [15] The truth is that God actualizes his liberation of people through the responsive and cooperative *action* of that people.

Rethinking the biblical concept of the kingdom of God from the perspective of Black liberation leads one to the following conclusions. It is both irrelevant and harmful for Black folk to spend time

---

[14] Robert A. Bennett, "Black Experience and the Bible," *New Theology No. 9,* ed. Martin E. Marty and Dean G. Peerman (New York: The Macmillan Company, 1972), p. 177.
[15] Wilmore, *op. cit.,* p. 152.

raising questions of when and where the kingdom of God is. Such discussion not only wastes precious time necessary to the Black struggle, but it also aids in the misunderstanding of the Hebraic-Christian tradition and the covenant faith. Blacks must *do* the kingdom. They must *act out* their side of the new covenant. They are to be *soldiers* of the cross, *not tourists* of it. William S. Douds wrote three decades ago: "But a king is a ruler. So then, the Kingdom of God is the rule of God. And his rule is his will. Hence, his Kingdom comes in just the measure that his will is *done* on earth as it is in heaven." [16]

When the people of God *do* the kingdom, that is, when they *act* on their covenant with Jesus Christ, God establishes his kingdom. When Black people in community commit themselves to the cross, take the risks, walk and work in jeopardy for Jesus' sake, there is always a resurrection of victory which follows. This is the shape of the kingdom. It is not to be located or awaited; it is to be *done.*

When the nature of the kingdom of God was thus understood in the struggle for civil rights, many Blacks in the liberation camp became eyewitnesses of its power in their midst. Paddy wagons and jails were filled. Evil laws were defied. Demonic principalities and powers were exposed and challenged. Men and women, Black, White, Protestant, Catholic, Jewish, Moslem, Hindu, and "atheist" marched in cadence with God, like the children of Israel around Jericho, until dehumanizing patterns crumbled. Thousands rode buses in his name. Lunch counters and hotels had to serve Black mouths while racist legislators helplessly watched. Black children sat in schoolrooms which many had vowed they would *never* occupy.

These all had been grasped by the kingdom's power. But more than this, the liberating God got into the international area to fight for Black liberation. Black ex-G.I.'s who had experienced the democracy of water-filled trenches in North Africa, France, Italy, Germany, Iwo Jima, Okinawa, Korea, and later Vietnam vowed to receive at home the "democracy" for which they ostensibly had fought. The Western White world was never the same. The winds of God's liberation swept over the colonies of Africa creating a reciprocal empathy between American Blacks and African Blacks.

It is no accident but Divine Providence that a war which really began when the dictator Benito Mussolini attacked Ethiopia, a Black

---

[16] William S. Douds, *Thy Kingdom Come—Why Not Now?* (Greenville, Pa.: The Beaver Press, 1942), p. 25. (Italics mine.)

nation, paved the way for the freedom of many African colonies. It is proof of the mysterious power of God that tyrants are often "hanged by the ropes which they spin." For, in their anti-Semitism, Mussolini and Adolf Hitler drove away·from their countries two Jews who eventually helped to perfect the atom bomb, Enrico Fermi and Albert Einstein. But more than this, the emergence of the nuclear age put all peoples on the same interdependent footing, White and Black. Hear the Black church when its members say:

> God moves in a mysterious way
> His wonders to perform;
> He plants his footsteps in the sea,
> And rides upon the storm.[17]

A search of the Gospels will show that Jesus believed several things about the kingdom of God and its nature. And what he said backs up what has been stated in the preceding paragraphs.

Jesus certainly believed that the kingdom and its power were not locational objects but represented an available power in the midst of a people to be acted upon: "The kingdom of God is not coming with signs to be observed; nor will they say, 'Lo, here it is!' or 'There!' for behold the kingdom of God is in the midst of you" (Luke 17:20-21). Yet he believed that it represented God's initiative. Note: "Fear not, little flock, for it is your Father's good pleasure to give you the kingdom" (Luke 12:32).

According to Jesus, rap sessions and prayer meetings without action will not blend with the kingdom: "Not every one who says to me, 'Lord, Lord,' shall enter the kingdom of heaven, but he who does the will of my Father who is in heaven" (Matthew 7:21). But, he went on to say, we must actively cultivate and harvest the kingdom's results. This is the meaning of the farmer's parable:

And he said, "The kingdom of God is as if a man should scatter seed upon the ground, and should sleep and rise night and day, and the seed should sprout and grow, he knows not how. The earth produces of itself, first the blade, then the ear, then the full grain in the ear. But when the grain is ripe, at once he puts in the sickle, because the harvest has come" (Mark 4:26-29).

Lastly, lest his hearers would fail to internalize the top priority of total allegiance to the kingdom and its liberation program, Jesus told these two parables:

[17] *The Baptist Hymnal* (Valley Forge: Judson Press, 1883), p. 81.

"The Kingdom of heaven is like a treasure hidden in a field. A man happens to find it, so he covers it up again. He is so happy that he goes and *sells everything* he has, and then goes back and buys the field."

"Also the Kingdom of heaven is like a buyer looking for fine pearls. When he finds one that is unusually fine, he goes and *sells everything* he has, and buys the pearl" (Matthew 13:44-46, TEV, italics added).

There is nothing more important than the kingdom and its liberation program. They take priority over *everything* and demand and deserve total Black action and allegiance.

Questions for Further Study

1. According to biblical witness, what is the real "tap-root" of sin?
2. What arguments are used to prove that the Bible teaches world abandonment by the church? To prove world affirmation, redemption, and liberation?
3. What does the Bible teach about the concept of the kingdom of God, and what implication does that teaching have for the Black struggle?
4. What is the relationship between the nature of the covenant and the nature of the "kingdom" concept when both are viewed through Black eyes?

Additional Reading

Cone, James H., *A Black Theology of Liberation* (Philadelphia: J. B. Lippincott Company, 1970).

Cox, Harvey, *God's Revolution and Man's Responsibility* (Valley Forge: Judson Press, 1965).

Manson, T. W., *The Servant-Messiah* (Cambridge, England: Cambridge University Press, 1953).

Williams, Colin, *Where in the World?* (New York: National Council of Churches of Christ, 1963).

Wilmore, Gayraud, *The Secular Relevance of the Church* (Philadelphia: The Westminster Press, 1962).

A Word to the Black Church

5

Any word of admonition to the Black church should be prefaced with the reminder that the very existence of a *Black* church resulted from the fact that American Christianity never fully came to grips with the issue of race in this country. In American White Christianity, as a whole, the preoccupation with expediency and privilege, and a deep conviction that somehow and in some way Whites were better than Blacks overshadowed the resolve to follow the full implication of the Hebraic-Christian faith. When the question of whether Christianizing a Black slave granted him or her legal freedom arose, the official answer in many sections of the country was "no." In that decision Jesus Christ was once again crucified. The Black church came into being in America when the American church, like Simon Peter, denied its Lord.

During the early days of the country, even in those sections where Black slavery was not held in high premium and racial segregation was somewhat relaxed, de facto racism was encountered as a daily fact, even in the churches. Richard Allen and Absalom Jones were not agitators who received pleasure from interrupting the peace and calm of the congregations in which they were worshiping. They and their sympathizers separated themselves because of the subtle racist policies under which they were made to worship. The Black church emerged because the American White church betrayed its prophetic heritage.

In the southernmost section of the country, the story of what happened is well known. There the attempt was made to convince people that God had rubber-stamped the institution of Black slavery. In this effort many Southern congregations became dominant partners. How could Blacks worship a God pictured in the Bible as Liberator in congregations which taught that Blacks must forever live under forced toil and painful whiplash? This question assumes, of course, that Blacks were even granted permission to attend services in these Southern congregations. Actually, studies show that after the 1800s Blacks were increasingly barred from White church congregations and only Black house servants and baby-sitters were allowed in at all.

In both North and South, Blacks were driven out of the congregations by forces and circumstances not of their own making. There is certainly irony in the fact that the very institution claiming to be God's "salt of the earth" itself fell prey to Satan's arrows of racism.

So Black people need not feel either apologetic or ashamed that there is now a Black church in America. Rather they should rejoice under the circumstances. For not only does the existence of the Black church stand as an indictment of American Christianity's failure, but also it is an organ of prophetic protest and an agent for helping Black people through many struggling years.

As one who has had the privilege of both serving and being served by the Black Church, I want to offer a word to it relative to today's quest for Black liberation.

Your Awesome Responsibility

Never has the responsibility of the Black church been so crucial and so heavy as it is today. Yet it could evade its God-given task by being too misdirected, too timid, and too brainwashed. Without taking seriously its Lord's mandate, it could become a closed, self-serving, institutionalized, good-feeling society dedicated to sanctifying the status quo on Sunday morning instead of "healing the broken-hearted," applying the gospel to the poor, and working for the liberation of the hurt and enslaved.

It ought to be common knowledge that the Black church in America has always performed a multiple function for its people.

Men like W. E. B. DuBois, E. Franklin Frazier, and Charles S. Johnson in their lifetime never ceased to point out that fact. Aside from the most obvious and expected role of spiritual uplift it assumed, the Black church functioned as an agent of social, political, and economic benefits and outlet for Black people. The benefits and outlets denied to Blacks in the wider community in the past were provided by the Black church.

Not many years ago few Black church members could run for political office on any level, could work in the tax collection office, or could serve on a board which determined the direction or recipients of social services. Few Blacks had a hand in the shaping of the policies of money lending and financing agencies and institutions. But in the Black congregation the member who had toiled all week without praise or voice and with scant pay could become chairman of the Board of Deacons, raise and deposit the collection, direct the missionary effort of helping the "sick and shut-ins," and determine the projects to be embraced by his or her own community, the Black congregation.

It is no riddle that Black people inside and outside the institutional Black church who are in any appreciable degree sensitive to the present Black struggle look to the Black church for words of hope and encouragement, for some workable strategies and directions, as well as for financial help.

Therefore, the Black church now has laid in its lap, so to speak, tremendous responsibility and opportunity. It has the responsibility and opportunity in a time of great need not only to do more of what it has done in the past for Black survival, but it has also the awesome mandate to make a shift of emphasis from "Black survival" to "Black liberation." How well the Black church in America accepts and honors this divine mandate will determine both its own image in the eyes of the struggling, Black masses and the degree to which America will be humanely shaped. If the Black church fails, it will lose its divine credentials. If it does not truly follow its Lord, God will remove his divine lampstand from its midst in accordance with the warning to the church at Ephesus delivered by the author of Revelation: "But I have this against you, that you have abandoned the love you had at first. Remember then from what you have fallen, repent and do the works you did at first. If not, I will come to you and remove your lampstand from its place, unless you repent" (Revelation 2:4 and 5).

Your Strategic Position

God's commissioned and anointed people are always in a strategic position, the right spot, when they are surrounded by human misery, sorrow, and suffering. For it is the task of God's church to do battle against the evils which plague God's children. However, aside from the position faced by God's anointed generally, the Black church enjoys a uniquely strategic position due to several developments.

It was noted earlier that the Black church was forced into being, one might say, as an island haven for Black people. It became a society within a society, taking care of Black needs. As a result it became the main occasion for Black togetherness, and it still is today. It also became the biggest Black platform. It housed the most effective Black leadership, and still does, aside from the debate as to whether that leadership is relevant or not. Moreover, the Black church has been the freest institution Blacks have had and perhaps the only one which they could rightly call their own.

Even those Blacks who have, for whatever reasons good or bad, slackened their childhood embrace of the Black institutional church still concede its advantages of having Black leadership, Black assembly, a good degree of community cohesion, and a better-than-average communications system for the community. Black politicians will still go to it to make appeals and solicit its support. Black community leaders and Black educators regard it as worthy of receiving important announcements. Often initial support for worthy Black community projects is generated in the Black congregations. The Montgomery Movement and the O.I.C. are good examples.

It is no accident that much of the Black leadership of the slave rebellions was Black-church based. It is noteworthy that Gabriel Prosser and Nat Turner were Black preachers. It may be well known that Denmark Vessey, Frederick Douglass, David Walker, Harriet Tubman, and Sojourner Truth were ardent, Black church members. God's Black colony has always been and is now in an extraordinarily strategic position to aid the struggle of Black liberation.

Shed Your Feeling of Inferiority

Let us be honest and admit that there was and is a systematic and systemic effort in this country to brainwash everything Black into believing that it is inferior. The Black church has been no exception.

In my boyhood days leaders and writers, Black and White, paused to take slaps at the Black church. They said that its leadership was not educated enough, that its services were too emotional, too long, and too otherworldly. They criticized its record keeping and the inadequacies of its Sunday school. They claimed that it did not undergird the morality of its members.

In short, they all implied that the Black church, to be viable, effective, and influential, must imitate the White church and use White criteria in theology (concept of God), ethics (right treatment of others), liturgy (church service), polity (church organization), and homiletics (theory of preaching). The truth of the matter is that upon close examination the advice that the Black church ought to imitate the White church is faulty on several accounts.

First, the African psychoreligious roots of the Black American may not be so easily blended with White religious folkways. Black scholars more recently have asserted that the loud call-and-response participation in Black congregations has its roots in Africa. Gayraud Wilmore taped African ceremonies and played them alongside Black American congregational singing. The similarities were amazing. What we know as traditional Black preaching and the "amen" responses to it have features similar to the African tribal chief's call and the response from the members of the group.

Another related feature of African rootage is the now known fact that Africans, in their love for life in its totality, often employ gestures and rhythm as well as sounds and words to convey and symbolize their meaning. This practice has tended to make less mysterious and, one might add, more acceptable in Western eyes the freedom of movement and outcry one encounters in Black church services.

There was once a tendency to call this freedom of movement and free-flowing emotion a sign of ignorance and unrefinement. And many Blacks, wanting to please, worried about their image in the White mind. This concern is gradually diminishing, and should do so. The White church has no monopoly on divine criteria by which church services should be conducted. All in all, it is unlikely that there is to be a complete blending of the Black and White ways of shaping church services in the near future.

A second reason that the advice to the Black church to pattern after the White church will not stand up is that the two churches have radically different theological perspectives. That is to say that their conceptions of God are different. One thing that twentieth-century theology has made clear through the minds of Paul Tillich and others is that one's conception of God is unavoidably given shape at least in part by one's situation, problems, interests, and hopes. For this reason, the White church and the Black church cannot see God with the same eyes. The Black church looks at God from a down-under position. The White church by the very nature of the favored position of its members looks at God from an on-top position.

It is either theologically naive or patently dishonest to claim that the oppressed will perceive God in the same manner as will the oppressor. It should be clear why most White churches in America tend to see even the God pictured in the Bible as a protector of the status quo, a divine law-and-order champion, or as one who automatically sanctifies private property, free enterprise, individual initiative, the president of the United States, and "America right or wrong."

Blacks, on the other hand, by the nature of their condition in America, must envision God as a Rescuer, a Liberator, One who heals the hurt and feeds the have-nots. Incidentally, this conception of God is closer to the biblical conception.

Thirdly, the advice to use the White church as a model is bogus when one views the history of the failure of the White church to make its own members just and humane to Black people. It is no secret that right up to the middle sixties there were White churches proclaiming that God ordained racial segregation. Neither is it unknown that the existence of evangelistic crusades in this country failed to halt the resurgence of the Ku Klux Klan, the rise of White Citizens' Councils, and the corruption known as Watergate.

The Black church therefore should shed its sense of inferiority caused by years of White brainwashing. It should remember the beauty, efficacy, and power of its spirituals, congregational hymns, poetic and spontaneous prayers, and its pulpit statesmen. If the shape of a people's response to God serves human needs and at the same time avoids hurting human beings, this is the only criterion necessary. The church's main concerns should be theology and ethics and not aesthetics and academic status.

Reemphasize the Nature and Task of the True Church

Someone once wisely observed that the true church of Jesus Christ is one which imitates its Lord in all things. Genuine Christians are quick to point out that God "sent" his only begotten Son into the world to redeem and liberate humankind. It stands to reason, then, that the church is composed of the "sent ones." These sent ones "go" where the wretched are, where the misery is, to find the "lost sheep," to seek and to save the lost of all manners and shapes.

Gayraud Wilmore quotes Alexander Crummell, the great Black abolitionist preacher, as saying: "We should let our godliness exhale like the odor of flowers. We should live for the good of our kind, and strive for the salvation of the world."[1] The intent and the aim of the Black church should certainly be no less than this at this crucial point in our history.

The genuine church—and the Black church must be genuine—operates basically not in self-interest but "for others," particularly for the needy others. In recent years much attention has been given to Dietrich Bonhoeffer's view of the church expressed in the statement: "The Church is her true self only when she exists for humanity."[2] For the Black church in these days this means in plain words that it must spend itself on behalf of the oppressed, the poor, the maltreated, and the helpless. The Black church must be ever restless, disturbed, dissatisfied, and uncomfortable as long as there are groups, forces, systems, structures, and circumstances which crush human beings. The essence of genuine church membership is to "go" into the world and help the disinherited and the helpless. Who can empathize with these people more than the Black church?

Specific Tasks of the Black Church

Reuben A. Sheares II has pointed out that the general task of the Black church is the liberation of Black people.[3] However, lest there be some question about the specific application of this task in its relevant concreteness, here are some specific ways in which the Black church can enhance Black liberation. Keep in mind that the Black church has always addressed these areas. The plea now is that more be done in these realms.

One area in which Black liberation can be aided is that of Black aspiration. The Black church has always been and must now be even more the great inspirer. In the midst of disillusionment and often cynicism, it somehow convinced a large number of its members that "God was still on the throne," that he cared, and that he could be

---

[1] Gayraud Wilmore, *Black Religion and Black Radicalism* (Garden City: Doubleday & Company, Inc., 1972), p. 159.
[2] Dietrich Bonhoeffer, *Letters and Papers from Prison,* ed. Eberhard Bethge (New York: The Macmillan Company, 1962), p. 239.
[3] Cf. Reuben A. Sheares II, "Beyond White Theology," *Christianity and Crisis,* November 2 and 16, 1970, pp. 230-234.

counted on to "move in good time." From its doors the Black members emerged singing:

> God moves in a mysterious way
> His wonders to perform;
> He plants his footsteps in the sea,
> And rides upon the storm.[4]

The Black church taught with effect that no injustice or evil, however deeply entrenched, would ultimately defeat the God who rescued Israel from Egypt and who raised Jesus from the dead. It taught with such fervor and passion that God would "change things" and "make a way out of no way" that the average member caught up in the congregational drama of the *mysterium tremendum** was penetrated by hope.

The Black church as great inspirer of Black people must now intensify its role, for there are many Blacks today who could lose heart in the midst of the struggle for liberation. If this should happen, it would be a very real form of enslavement. To inspire Blacks is to contribute in a very real way to their liberation.

Another realm in which Black liberation can receive help is that of the minds and emotions of Black people. Note that the New Testament has much to say about demon-possession or being possessed with devils. The realities to which that ancient wording points are still with us today. In other words, there are demons of the minds and emotions of oppressed people which form mental and emotional chains just as real in their effect as physical chains.

Yes, the Black church has been and must remain in a more intensified way an exorcist. This exorcism is not meant in the usual sensationalized sense found in certain movies. What is pictured here is the less spectacular, everyday instance of freeing people whose will and motivation are sapped by fear, distrust, self-deprecation, and docility under oppression. Paulo Freire, in his book *Pedagogy of the Oppressed,*[5] focuses on this strange but real phenomenon. Many Black scholars and Christian educators are emphasizing that this task of mental and emotional exorcism should be the main concern of the Black Sunday school. The Black child born into an environment which negates his or her being, and the child's well-being needs such a service.

---

[4] *The Baptist Hymnal* (Valley Forge: Judson Press, 1883), p. 81.
[5] Paulo Freire, *Pedagogy of the Oppressed* (New York: The Seabury Press, Inc., 1973).

These demons in the Black mind are real. When Black children or adults hate themselves, that is a demon. When Black persons swallow without rebellion the notion that Blacks can neither know nor do as well as Whites, that is a demon. When Blacks fear to assert their rights, their worth, and their potential, there is a demon to be cast out. And, when these demons are cast out, their God-given opposites, such as faith, hope, and self-affirmation as children of God, must replace them. The Black church has always performed this function and must continue to so do at a greater pace.

Still another side of the freedom task has to do with feeding, clothing, sheltering, and educating the needy. The Black church has always known that for the needy, Black masses mere sermon delivery was not enough, that it had to minister to the whole person. As it matured in its role, the Black church knew that it had to be an economic conduit for its people. It realized that it had to find financial help for its people and use it with honesty and equity.

Often such help took strange forms. Burial societies were formed. Lodges with close connection with the institutional church emerged. Traveling mission groups came into being.

More recently, units of the Black church have served as receiving agencies of federal and philanthropic funding of community projects and community action groups. And despite heavy criticism, Black churches have met human needs where they found them. The Black church must on a wider scale remain an "economic conduit" for Black people. This is a vital part of the liberation journey.

Lastly, one of the functions which the Black church had from its beginning performed with varying degrees of intensity was that of a "change agent." Much of the anger directed toward the Black church's identification with the civil rights movements of the late fifties and sixties came about because many had forgotten the Black church's freedom involvement in the abolition activities, the slave rebellions, and the Reconstruction period.

Today, many Black liberation soldiers of the past are spoken of as if they were isolated, self-styled fanatics with touches of insanity. The truth is that the vast majority of them were associated with the Black church and received their inspiration and direction from their understanding of the Christian faith.

The Black church has been and is the greatest change agent Black people have had. It has been and is the greatest foe of racial discrimination despite some timid souls within it. It supported voter registration efforts. In spite of White rage and the fiery torch, it opened its basements to N.A.A.C.P. meetings in the dangerous fifties. It taught its members the distinction between the cross of the Ku Klux Klan and the cross of Jesus Christ. And most of all, it taught its people that racist politicians were not God Almighty.

Moreover, who can forget or ignore the Black church-based movements associated with such names as Leon Sullivan, Martin Luther King, Jr., and Albert Cleage, to name just a few? The forty-year period of relative Black church slumber from 1900 to 1940 caused many Americans to forget that groups of Black folk believing in the power of God have formed the greatest force for change American society has ever known. Let today's Black church be aware of this and resolve to carry the baton for the last lap, so to speak.

This concludes the word to the Black church from one who has always cherished its inspiration and guidance and who will always love it. My prayer now is that the Black church will be as faithful in this era of "Black liberation" as it was in the past era of "Black survival."

Questions for Further Study

1. Why was a Black church made necessary in America?
2. Why are some Blacks suspicious of the advice to Black congregations to imitate and pattern after White congregations?
3. Do White seminaries' homiletics departments really know Black preaching? Why or why not?
4. What are the reasons for developing a Black theology in contrast to a White theology in America?
5. What has the Black church generally seen as its task in the past and how must it see its task now?

Additional Reading

Cleage, Albert B., Jr., *The Black Messiah* (New York: Sheed & Ward, Inc., 1968).

Frazier, E. Franklin, *The Negro Church in America* (New York: Schocken Books, Inc., 1964).

Hiltner, Seward, *Pastoral Counseling* (Nashville: Abingdon Press, 1949).

King, Martin Luther, Jr., "Letter from a Birmingham Jail," *Why We Can't Wait* (New York: Harper & Row, Publishers, 1964).

Mitchell, Henry H., *Black Preaching* (Philadelphia: J. B. Lippincott Co., 1970).

Sidran, Ben, *Black Talk* (New York: Holt, Rinehart and Winston, Inc., 1971).

Sullivan, Leon H., *Build Brother Build* (Philadelphia: Macrae Smith Company, 1969).

Woodson, Carter G., *The History of the Negro Church* (Washington, D.C.: The Associated Publishers, 1921).

Conclusion

The main aim of this book is to urge and, in some small degree, to help the rank and file of Black Americans to rediscover the biblical message and its liberating power. The method behind this aim, if it has been successful, has been to uncover the kinds of tampering with the true biblical message which have occurred in the past, and at the same time to afford a glimpse of the proper way to approach the Bible and the liberating rewards which this affords.

The central conviction running through the book is that the Bible's chief faith-admonition is that men and women, particularly the suffering and enslaved, are called to work with a God who frees, empowers, and heals those who venture into a covenant relationship with him. Black Americans have known and are presently experiencing forces, structures, systems, principalities, and powers which deny their humanity and place in the sun.

The hope is that Blacks in greater numbers in America will rediscover the Bible and avail themselves of the power and direction in this "liberation time" which many of their foreparents found in "survival time." The covenant relationship between the liberating God and an oppressed people is a call-and-response relationship in which the people's freedom obedience meets God's offer of freedom power and direction. This cannot be a one-way street. Someone in this connection has used the illustration of steam as a source of power to make the point. Both the heat and the liquid must come together before the actualized power is released.

Glossary of Terms

Every branch of human knowledge, every area of expertise, and every division of labor has its own pet language. Not only does an area coin new terms to express what it is about (and sometimes to protect itself), but also an area often will use common terms in different ways. The areas of biblical and theological studies are no different.

In view of this fact, here is an effort to define and explain some words and terms which appear in this work.

Aetiology or etiology

This term has to do with the science or theory of causes and reasons behind the existence of something. In the area of biblical studies, the term is used relative to questions raised by biblical writers, such as to the origin of creation, the human race, multiple languages, different peoples, evil, and human conflict. Often ancient people explained the reasons for these in story form, such as the story (in Genesis 11:1-9) of the confusion of tongues at the tower of Babel.

Allegory (allegorical—adjective form)

An allegory is a fictional narrative which is told to get across to the hearers a moral truth or a principle to live by. For instance, John Bunyan's *Pilgrim's Progress* is an allegory.

Apocalyptic

"Apocalyptic" is a term descriptive of thought patterns, literature, conditions, and human activity which usually emerge out of periods of great hostility, persecution, oppression, and turbulence experienced by a people. Such a period is usually pregnant with both strong foreboding and great effort to see the divine design in the midst of the chaotic conditions. More often than not, such a time plunges people into a realistic dependence upon deep spiritual resources and thus produces tremendous heroism. "Apocalyptic" times are those in which the forces of evil are on a collision course with God so that the ultimate victory of good is assured. Liberation of oppressed people is such a good.

Atheist

This term is usually used in a broad sense to refer to a person who does not believe in the reality of God. The Greek word for God is "theos," and the English word for one who believes in God is "theist." The Greeks often used their first alphabet letter, the alpha (a), to form a negative prefix. So atheos is one who denied the gods. In English, atheist is one who does not believe in God.

Baal—Baalim (pl.)

This is the name of the chief god of the Canaanite pantheon (group of gods arranged in terms of authority levels). The name is pronounced like the words "bale" or "bail." Since fertility of animals, orchards, and grain constituted the main principle in agricultural Canaan's religious system, the gods were often thought of in terms of males with female mates. Baal's mate was Astarte.

Canaan—Canaanite (inhabitant)

This is an area in the Palestinian strip, a piece of land which joins Africa and Asia. To this area the wandering Israelites came after having escaped bondage in Egypt. Economic life in Canaan during the Israelite settlement was mainly settled and basically agricultural. Social life in Canaan was very individualistic and materialistic. Every person cared for himself or herself only and saw material possession as the highest good for which to strive. Religion in Canaan was regarded as a way of bribing the gods into doing favors for humans.

Confederacy

A "confederacy" is a cooperative relationship between or among several parties often involving mutual protection and other benefits. The relationship usually revolves around something held in common, such as an idea, land borders, or the need to repel a common danger. One may note that the early Israelite confederacy was held together by common ancestry, common heritage, and a common religious faith.

Covenant

In the most general sense, a covenant is a solemn agreement or contract between two parties, sometimes of equal rank and other times of unequal rank, in which each party pledges something to the other. In the covenant between God and Israel (unequal parties), God took the initiative by virtue of what he had already done for Israel in rescuing her from Egypt and guiding her through the wilderness to the Promised Land. In this covenant God pledged, as proven in his prior action, liberation, guidance, and cohesion. Israel in turn pledged total obedience and total recognition of God's sovereignty and ethical conduct. When one party violates its end of a covenant, the agreement is broken. However, in the case of the covenant between God and Israel, God remained merciful in spite of Israel's violation and urged Israel's repentance as an avenue to reconciliation.

Demon

Many ancients believed that invisible beings roamed the earth as agents of evil. These people believed that these beings often entered human beings and controlled their behavior. Such beings were often referred to as demons or devils.

Exile

Generally the word "exile" means to be banished or "put out" of a place. In the area of biblical studies, it more often than not means that period in the existence of the Hebrew nations, Judah and Israel, when they were conquered by Assyria and Babylonia.

Faith portrait

"Faith portrait" is a term used in biblical studies to explain that the Gospels in the New Testament were written by persons who wrote not primarily to report religious events but to picture what their religious faith saw and sensed in the story of Jesus.

Genocide

"Genocide" is a term which means the act of heaping death or destruction upon a particular people in a deliberate effort.

Group solidarity

This term is often employed to mean a society in which there is a high degree of group unity and mutual compassion and justice. In such a society the interdependence factor is greatly recognized.

Kingdom of God (sometimes referred to as the kingdom of heaven)

It is now reasonably agreed upon by biblical and theological scholars that Jesus used the concept to mean a kind and quality of earthly society in which God is acknowledged as King or Sovereign; a quality of corporate human relations in which God's will for humility, justice, and compassion is actualized. The concept has roots in Old Testament times and was regarded by Jesus and the early church as having been in some sense fulfilled and intensified in Jesus' ministry, death, and resurrection.

Legend

A legend is a story told over and over for its value to the spirit or memory of a group. It may have a core of historical fact, but often the nonhistorical details gathered around it over the years have hidden the historical events.

Messiah (messianic, adj. form)

The name is given to the divine agent which the Israelites expected God to send to earth to rescue and redeem his people and signal earthly renewal. Later a group of Jews proclaimed Jesus of Nazareth as this agent. Through the action and testimony of this group, many non-Jews came to hold the same conviction. The group became known as Christians or the church.

Millenarians

This term is generally used with reference to a variety of groups who believe that they have by calculation, determined the time when God will historically consummate his rule on earth. Many of these persons base their beliefs on their view of Revelation 20:1-5.

Mysterium tremendum

"Mysterium tremendum" in a shallow definition can be interpreted as an experience of God as a tremendous or great mystery. But a deeper understanding of what the expression gets at dictates that one is here attempting to express the inexpressible, namely the experience of God's holiness, the divine-human encounter. While this experience is not against the rational in man, it goes beyond the rational. It is like the faith affirmation expounded by the Book of Job. God gives Job no rational answers but gives Job genuine encounter with the Divine.

Myth

A term often misunderstood in biblical research efforts because of one of its general definitions, myth has a definitely useful function. It puts into story form the answers to the vast experiences, questions, and quests of human existence. In this sense, myth is a bit akin to the parable and personified literature. Yet because one of the popular definitions of myth is "a false belief or opinion," to use the term in biblical studies tends to "turn some people off."

Orthodox

"Orthodox" is a term given to what is regarded as proper, correct, expected, and permitted.

The Passover

The Passover is the religious ritual instituted by Moses and the Israelites just prior to the Exodus from Egypt. It became a central rite in Israel. In its original nature it involved the eating of roasted lamb, unleavened bread, and bitter herbs, each symbolizing religious meaning for that group.

It is believed in many Christian circles that the Lord's Supper was an abbreviated version of the Passover.

Patriarch

This is a term applied to the absolute head of a clan or a community. Abraham is often called the patriarch of the Israelites.

Placate

To placate one is to appease one, to make one happy or satisfied in order to receive a favor or friendship from one.

Prometheus

In Greek mythology, Prometheus defied the gods and drew fire from the heavens. The term "Promethean" is often used to describe those who defy deity.

Racism

This is a term given to any sustained pattern or system of beliefs and actions directed against another group based solely on that group's race or color.

Resurrection

"Resurrection" is the reference to the revival of something or someone. In the Christian faith it is a term affirming that God raised Jesus from death. Note that the Christian faith at its core affirms that Jesus *was dead,* not in some trance nor possessed of some sort of immortal soul. Immortality is not a New Testament concept. Jesus was dead, and God raised him from the *dead.*

Rites

These are acts and gestures done periodically in connection with group observance of religious, fraternal, or patriotic convictions.

Saga

A saga is a story packed full of risk and adventure and often showing human victory—often told to inspire courage similar to that recounted.

Samaritan

A Samaritan was a citizen of one of the three provinces of Palestine during the days of Jesus. Because the province, Samaria, was populated by Jews who had intermarried with non-Jews, it was scorned and avoided. A Samaritan was a "half-breed" in the eyes of the orthodox keepers of the ancient Israelite faith. Jesus, in his distaste for bigotry, used every opportunity to paint this hated citizen as a hero.

Second Isaiah (sometimes written II Isaiah)

Many biblical scholars today have agreed that the book of Isaiah in the Old Testament was written by more than one author. They point out that research shows that the author of chapters 1–39 is not the author of the rest of the book. Therefore chapters 40–66 are called Second Isaiah.

Semites (Semitic, adj. form)

This term refers to a people of which the Hebrews or Israelites were a part. Often today we note that the word anti-Semitism is used to denote the kind of thinking which irrationally hates Jews and makes them scapegoats.

Sovereignty

The term "sovereignty" means having complete mastery, with unquestioned right and power to rule.

Wisdom Literature

Wisdom Literature is a term referring to such poetic biblical writings as Proverbs and Ecclesiastes. It received its name from the fact that it emphasizes directions for practical, everyday living, for commonsense wisdom.

World Abandonment

World abandonment refers to a religious or theological conviction, latent or active, which affirms that the alienation between God and the created order (this world) is so deep and strong that God has withdrawn from the world and marked it for ultimate and total destruction. Persons holding such a conviction reason, therefore, that to emulate God they, too, must withdraw from such an "evil and cursed" world and repudiate any effort at earthly reform. Such efforts would be both sinful and useless, they maintain. For Black liberation such a view is a "cop-out."

Bibliography

Books

Anderson, Bernhard W., *The Living World of the Old Testament.*
London: Longmans, Green and Co., Ltd., 1957.
————————, *Understanding the Old Testament.* Englewood Cliffs,
N.J.: Prentice Hall, Inc., 1957.

Augustine, *City of God.* New York: E. P. Dutton & Co., Inc., n.d.

Bonhoeffer, Dietrich, *Letters and Papers from Prison.* New York:
The Macmillan Company, 1953.

Buswell, James O. III, *Slavery, Segregation and Scripture.* Grand
Rapids, Mich.: William B. Eerdmans Publishing Co., 1963.

Charles, R. H., *The Book of Enoch.* Oxford: Clarendon Press, 1912.

Cleage, Albert B., Jr., *The Black Messiah.* New York: Sheed & Ward,
Inc., 1969.

Cone, James H., *Black Theology and Black Power.* New York: The Seabury Press, Inc., 1969.

Cox, Harvey, *God's Revolution and Man's Responsibility.* Valley Forge: Judson Press, 1965
_____, *The Secular City.* New York: The Macmillan Company, 1966.

Craig, Clarence Tucker, *Beginning of Christianity.* New York: Abingdon-Cokesbury Press, 1943.

Dabbs, James McBride, *Haunted by God.* Richmond, Va.: John Knox Press, 1972.

Darwin, Charles, *The Origin of Species.* New York: P. F. Collier and Son, 1909 (first edition Nov. 24, 1859).

Dodd, C. H., *Parables of the Kingdom.* New York: Charles Scribner's Sons, 1936.

Douds, William S., *Thy Kingdom Come . . . Why Not Now?* Greenville, Pa.: The Beaver Press, 1940.

DuBois, W. E. B., *The Souls of Black Folk.* New York: Washington Square Press, 1903.

Enslin, Morton Scott, *Christian Beginnings.* New York: Harper & Row, Publishers, 1938.

Fosdick, Harry Emerson, *Jesus of Nazareth.* New York: Random House, Inc., 1959.
_____, *The Man from Nazareth.* New York: Harper & Row, Publishers, 1949.

Franklin, John Hope, *From Slavery to Freedom.* New York: Alfred A. Knopf, Inc., 1967.

Fitzhugh, George, *Sociology for the South or the Failure of Free Society.* New York: Burt Franklin, 1965.

Fredrickson, George M., *The Black Image in the White Mind.* New York: Harper & Row, Publishers, 1971.

Goodspeed, Edgar J., *An Introduction to the New Testament.* Chicago: The University of Chicago Press, 1937.

Grant, Frederick C., *An Introduction to New Testament Thought.* New York: Abingdon Press, 1950.

Grant, Joanne, ed., *Black Protest.* Greenwich, Conn.: Fawcett Publications, Inc., 1968.

Grant, Robert M., *A Short History of the Interpretation of the Bible.* New York: The Macmillan Company, 1963.

Haselden, Kyle, *The Racial Problem in Christian Perspective.* New York: Harper & Row, Publishers, 1959.

Hertz, J. H., ed., *The Pentateuch and Haftorahs.* New York: Bloch Publishing Co., Inc., n.d.

Hester, Hubert I., *The Heart of Hebrew History.* Liberty, Mo.: William Jewell Press, 1949.

Hyatt, James P., *Prophetic Religion.* New York: Abingdon Cokesbury Press, 1947.

Jordan, Clarence, *The Cotton Patch Version of Paul's Epistles.* New York: Association Press, 1968.

Kelsey, George D., *Racism and the Christian Understanding of Man.* New York: Charles Scribner's Sons, 1965.

Lincoln, C. Eric, *The Black Muslims in America,* rev. ed. Boston: Beacon Press, 1973.

Manson, T. W., *The Servant-Messiah.* Cambridge, England: Cambridge University Press, 1953.

Maston, T. B., *The Bible and Race.* Nashville, Tenn.: Broadman Press, 1959.

Mould, Elmer W. K., *Essentials of Bible History.* New York: The Ronald Press Company, 1939.

Newby, I. A., *Jim Crow's Defense: Anti-Negro Thought in America, 1900-1930.* Baton Rouge: Louisiana State University Press, 1965.

Phillips, J. B., *Letters to Young Churches.* London: Geoffrey Bles, 1948.

Rasmussen, Albert T., *Christian Social Ethics.* Englewood Cliffs, N.J.: Prentice-Hall, Inc., 1956.

Rauschenbusch, Walter, *Christianizing the Social Order.* New York: The Macmillan Company, 1912.
_____, *Christianity and the Social Crisis.* New York: The Macmillan Company, 1907.
_____, *The Social Principles of Jesus.* Philadelphia: The American Baptist Publication Society, 1916.
_____, *A Theology for the Social Gospel.* Nashville: Abingdon Press, copyright renewal 1945.

Roberts, J. Deotis, *Liberation and Reconciliation: A Black Theology.* Philadelphia: The Westminster Press, 1971.

Robinson, John A. T., *In the End, God.* London: James Clarke and Co., Ltd., 1950.

Scott, Ernest F., *Literature of the New Testament.* New York: Columbia University Press, 1936.

Scott, R. B. Y., *The Relevance of the Prophets,* rev. ed. New York: The Macmillan Company, 1969.

Smith, H. Shelton, *In His Image, but: Racism in Southern Religion, 1780-1910.* Durham, N.C.: Duke University Press, 1972.

Stanton, William, *The Leopard's Spots: Scientific Attitudes Toward Race in America.* Chicago: The University of Chicago Press, 1960.

Werkmeister, William H., *An Introduction to Critical Thinking,* rev. ed. Chicago: Johnson Publishing Co., Inc., 1957.

Wheelwright, Philip, *The Burning Fountain,* rev. ed. Bloomington, Ind.: The Indiana University Press, 1968.

Wilder, Amos N., *The Language of the Gospel.* New York: Harper & Row, Publishers, 1964.

Williams, Colin, *Where in the World?* New York: National Council of the Churches of Christ in the U.S.A., 1963.
_____, *What in the World.* Epworth, 1965.

Wilmore, Gayraud, *Black Religion and Black Radicalism.* Garden City, N.Y.: Doubleday & Company, Inc., 1972.

Woodson, Carter G., *The History of the Negro Church.* Washington, D.C.: The Associated Publishers, 1921.

Wood, H. G., *et al., The Kingdom of God and History.* New York: Willett, Clark and Company, 1938.

Articles

J. Christiaan Beker, "Biblical Theology Today," *New Theology No. 6,* ed. Martin C. Marty and Dean G. Peerman. New York: The Macmillan Company, 1969.

Robert A. Bennett, "Black Experience and the Bible," in *New Theology No. 9,* edited by Martin C. Marty and Dean G. Peerman. New York: The Macmillan Company, 1962.

James H. Cone, "Black Consciousness and the Black Church," *Christianity and Crisis,* Nov. 2 and 16, 1970.

Reuben A. Sheares II, "Beyond White Theology," *Christianity and Crisis,* Nov. 2 and 16, 1970.

Hayward Henry, Jr., "Toward a Religion of Revolution," *The Black Scholar,* December, 1970.

Preston N. Williams, "The Black Experience and Black Religion," *New Theology No. 8,* ed. Martin C. Marty and Dean G. Peerman. New York: The Macmillan Company, 1971.

Reference Works

James Hastings, ed., *Dictionary of the Bible.* New York: Charles Scribner's Sons, 1963.

The Interpreter's Dictionary of the Bible, Vol. A-D. Nashville: Abingdon Press, 1962.

The Interpreter's One-Volume Commentary on the Bible. Nashville: Abingdon Press, 1971.

The New Oxford Annotated Bible (R.S.V.) New York: Oxford University Press, 1973.

Index